THE SECOND WORLD WAR
1939 – 45

THE SECOND WORLD WAR

1939 - 45

Christine Hatt

Evans

First published in 2007 by Evans Brothers Limited
2A Portman Mansions
Chiltern Street
London, W1U 6NR

Printed in Dubai by Oriental Press

British Library Cataloguing in Publication Data

Hatt, Christine
   World War Two: 1939-1945. - (History in writing)
   1. World War, 1939-1945 - Juvenile literature
   I. Title
   940.5'3

ISBN 0237531941
ISBN 13- 9780237531942

Design – Neil Sayer
Editorial – Nicola Barber
Maps – Tim Smith
Consultant – Terry Charman, Historian in the Research and
Information Office, Imperial War Museum, London
Production – Jenny Mulvanny

Title page picture: The Battle of Kursk, 1943
Border: Concentration camp watchtowers and barbed wire

To find out more about the Second World War, try looking at
these websites:

http://www.iwm.org.uk (Imperial War Museum site)

http://www.bbc.co.uk/history/wwtwo.shtml (BBC website)

http://www.unicaen.fr/collectivite/memorial/index.htm
(Caen Memorial Museum)

**http://www.vuw.ac.nz/%7Eagsmith/847/resguide/
merrick/home.htm**
(Useful World War 2 web resource guide)

http://www.pro.gov.uk
(Public Record Office)

ACKNOWLEDGEMENTS

For permission to reproduce copyright material for the documents, the author
and publisher gratefully acknowledge the following:

page 6, 11, 35, 59 From *The Major International Treaties 1914-1973* by J.A.S.
Grenville, published in 1974 by Methuen & Co Ltd. Reprinted by permission of
David Higham Associates. **page 7, 17, 43, 55** From *The Past is Myself* by
Christabel Bielenberg, published by Transworld Publishers Ltd, a division of
the Random House Group Ltd. Copyright © *Christabel Bielenberg* 1984. All
rights reserved. **page 7** (top and bottom right) **33, 47** (bottom) From *The
Second World War in Europe* by S.P. Mackenzie, published in 1999 by
Addison Wesley Longman, a division of Pearson Education Ltd. **page 7**
(bottom left) From *Hiroshima* by John Hershey, published in 1966 by Hamish
Hamilton. Copyright © John Hershey, 1985. Reprinted by permission of
Penguin UK **page 9** From *The Storm of Steel – from the diary of a German
Storm-Troop Officer on the Western Front* by Ernst Junger, published in 1929
by Chatto & Windus. **page 13** From *The Origins of the Second World War* by
Victor Mallia-Milanes, published in 1987 by Macmillan Education Ltd. **page
15** From *The Weimar Republic Source Book*, edited by Anton Kaes, Martin Jay
and Edward Dimendberg, published in 1994 by University of California Press.
Reprinted by permission of the University of California Press. **page 19**
(bottom), **49** (bottom) From *The Railway Man: A POW's Searing Account of
War, Brutality, and Forgiveness* by Eric Lomax. Copyright © 1995 by Eric
Lomax. Used by permission of W. W. Norton & Company, Inc. Published by
in 1996 by Vintage. **page 21** From *The Memoirs of Field-Marshal the Viscount
Montgomery of Alamein* published in 1958 by Da Capo Press, Inc. **page 23**
From *Women's Letters in Wartime. 1450-1945*, edited by Eva Figes, published
by Pandora, an imprint of Harper Collins Publishers. **page 25** From *Memoirs -
Ten Years and Twenty Days* by Admiral Doenitz, published in 1958 by Bernhard
& Graefe. **page 27** Taken from *War Poems* by Christopher Martin, published in
1991 by Collins Educational, a division of Harper Collins Publishers. **page 29**
From *Jahrbuch des Auslands - Organisation der NSDAP, 1942.* **page 31** From
The Second World War by John Keegan, published in 1997 by Pimlico.
Copyright © 1989 John Keegan. Reproduced by permission of Sheil Land
Associates Ltd. **page 37, 51** From *The Good War: An Oral History of World War
Two* by Studs Terkel, published in 1985 by Hamish Hamilton. Copyright
©1985 by Studs Terkel. Reprinted by permission of Penguin UK. **page 39**
From *Midway: The Battle That Doomed Japan* (Tokyo, 1968) by M Fuchida
and M Okumiya. **page 41, 55** (bottom) From *The Second World War and its
aftermath* by Colin C Bayne-Jardine, published in 1987 by Addison Wesley
Longman, a division of Pearson Education Ltd. **page 45** From *Children's
Wartime Diaries* by Laurel Holliday, published by Judy Piatkus (Publishers)
Ltd. © Laurel Holliday, 1995. **page 49** (top) From *The Imperial War Museum
Book of Victory in Europe* by Julian Thompson. Copyright © Julian Thompson
and the Imperial War Museum 1994. **page 53** (top) From *The Imperial War
Museum Book of Victory in Europe* by Julian Thompson. Reprinted by

permission of Derrick Vernon. **page 53** (bottom) *Winter in the Morning: A
Young Girl's Life in the Warsaw Ghetto and Beyond. 1939-1945*, by Janina
Bauman, published by Virago. Reprinted by permission of Virago.

While very effort has been made to secure permission to use copyright
material, Evans Brothers apologise for any errors or omissions in the above
list and would be grateful for notification of any corrections to be included in
subsequent editions.

CONTENTS

LOOKING AT DOCUMENTS

When the First World War ended in 1918 (see page 8), the countries that had participated in this terrible conflict were determined that killing on such a scale should never be repeated. Yet just over 20 years later, the globe once again plunged into another devastating struggle – the Second World War. This time the fighting spread across much more territory and cost the lives of millions more men, women and children.

The Second World War considers many aspects of this global upheaval. It examines the war's causes and the steps that led to the outbreak of fighting in 1939. It details the course of the conflict in Western Europe, the USSR, Africa and the Pacific, and assesses the roles of the main Allies – Britain, the USA and the USSR – on one side, and the main Axis Powers – Germany, Italy and Japan – on the other. It describes, too, the experiences of civilians on the home fronts, resistance fighters, prisoners of war and Holocaust victims. Finally, it looks at the dramatic end of the war in 1945 and the Cold War that followed.

To bring this story to life, *The Second World War* uses a wide range of documents. They include official treaties, political speeches, propaganda posters, diaries, letters and military memoirs. You will also find extracts from some of the great literary works inspired by the war, and from the autobiographies of people who endured the six years of conflict. To make the documents easy to read, we have printed them in modern type. Difficult or old-fashioned words or phrases are explained in labels around the text. Photographs of the original documents, and of their authors, appear alongside some extracts.

When you are looking at a document, think carefully about its origins. Does it date from the start of the war, when the main fighting was in Western Europe, or later, when the conflict was raging on several fronts? Was it written in a battle zone or a government office? Has it been censored to remove secret information? Or is it propaganda, designed to spread the official version of the truth? What were the writer's political views and nationality? These and similar questions will help you to work out how reliable a document is likely to be. But remember that no single document can give a full picture of the Second World War, and that the more you read, the more you will understand.

On these pages are a few extracts from the documents used in this book. They have been selected to give you an idea of the variety of documents included, and to explain how and why some were written.

Political and legal documents created the official framework for the war and its aftermath. Their dry words often reveal important truths. For example, the harsh terms of the Treaty of Versailles (see page 11), imposed on Germany at the end of the First World War, help to explain why the Second World War began.

Article 232... The Allied and Associated Governments... require, and Germany undertakes, that she will make compensation for all damage done to the civilian population of the Allied and Associated Powers and to their property during the period of belligerency of each as an Allied or Associated Power against Germany...

What does this word mean? Some words and phrases in the documents are difficult to understand. Captions alongside the documents give explanations of highlighted areas of text. You can find out what **belligerency** means on page 11.

Personal diaries kept by men in the battle zones offer shocking insights into the grim reality of warfare. One German soldier recorded the slow starvation suffered by himself and his comrades in the ruins of Stalingrad, USSR (see page 33).

December 26. The horses have already been eaten. I would eat a cat... The soldiers look like corpses or lunatics, looking for something to put in their mouths. They no longer take cover from Russian shells; they haven't the strength to walk, run away and hide. A curse on this war!

Private letters are another important source of information about the war. This extraordinary note (see page 55) was written by a Japanese *kamikaze* pilot just before he set off on a suicide mission against an American ship in the Pacific Ocean.

I leave for the attack with a smile on my face. The moon will be full tonight. As I fly over the open sea off Okinawa I will choose the enemy ship that is to be my target.

I will show you that I know how to die bravely.

A young *kamikaze* pilot in July 1944

Many works of literature were inspired by the terrible events of the Second World War. The dropping of atomic bombs on Japan in 1945 prompted American writer John Hersey to write his book *Hiroshima* (see page 55).

Transcripts of the War Crimes Trials (1945-6) reveal the thoughts of many high-ranking Nazis. In this interview, the commandant of a concentration camp explained how he carried out mass murder (see page 47).

He was the only person making his way into the city; he met hundreds and hundreds who were fleeing, and every one of them seemed to be hurt in some way. The eyebrows of some were burned off and skin hung from their faces and hands. Others, because of pain, held their arms up as if carrying something in both hands.

...it was possible to exterminate up to 10,000 people in one 24-hour period... The killing itself took the least time... it was the burning that took all the time. The killing was easy; you didn't even need guards to drive them into the chambers; they just went in expecting to take showers and, instead of water, we turned on poison gas....

CHAPTER 1

ORIGINS
THE FIRST WORLD WAR

The tensions that led to the First World War began to develop in 1871, when over 30 small states united to create the German Empire. The new, strong Germany formed the Triple Alliance with Austria-Hungary and Italy in 1882. Wary of Germany's increasing power, Britain and France came to an agreement to help each other, known as the Entente Cordiale, in 1904.

Austria-Hungary ruled a fading empire. Its people included thousands of Slavs, many of them Serbs, who wanted independence. They were backed by the Slav states of Serbia and Russia. In 1907, Russia joined Britain and France against the Triple Alliance, forming the Triple Entente.

Then, in 1914, a Serb killed the heir to the Austro-Hungarian throne. Austria-Hungary blamed Serbia for the crime and declared war, as did its ally Germany. Russia entered the war on Serbia's side and was quickly joined by its Triple Entente partners, Britain and France. The First World War was under way.

The Allies (Britain, France and Russia) and the Central Powers (Germany and Austria-Hungary) both predicted that the fighting would be over before the year's end. But instead, Germany's invasion of Belgium and France led to stalemate and years of trench warfare, in which millions of men died as they fought repeatedly over the same territory. As time passed, more countries entered the war. Among them were Italy (1915) and the USA (1917), who joined the Allies, as well as Turkey (1914) and Bulgaria (1915), who took the Central Powers' side.

The number of fronts increased, too. Men fought not only on the Western Front in Belgium and France, but also on the Eastern Front in Russia, and in Italy, Greece, Turkey, the Middle East, Africa and the Pacific. The Eastern Front closed down in 1918, when Russia left the war after its Communist revolution. By late 1918, the Allies were forcing the Germans back along the Western Front. Facing defeat in battle and unrest at home (see box page 9), Germany's ruler, Kaiser Wilhelm II, abdicated. The new government (see page 14) then requested an armistice. The war ended when the armistice was signed on 11 November 1918.

The victorious Allies had to devise a peace settlement. A conference to discuss its terms began on 18 January 1919 in Paris. It was signed on 28 June 1919 in the grand setting of the Palace of Versailles, just outside the city.

This painting shows American troops on a ship in the English port of Southampton. They were on their way to fight the First World War in mainland Europe, where about 2 million soldiers from the USA served.

Ernst Jünger was a German soldier who went to war in 1914, at the age of just 19. He served bravely in many battles on the Western Front and kept a diary of his experiences. In 1929, it was published in English as *The Storm of Steel*. These extracts highlight Jünger's love of his country and his determination to act with both courage and honour.

Ernst Jünger as an old man

THE 'STAB IN THE BACK'

By 1918, war casualties, severe food shortages and discontent with the Kaiser's regime had all prompted demonstrations and strikes in Germany. Army leader Erich Ludendorff used this situation to his advantage. Once it was clear that the final attack on the Allies had failed, he claimed that the army had been 'stabbed in the back' by lack of support from the civilian population. He also ensured that the new government, not the army, negotiated the armistice. The 'stab in the back' theory was believed by many First World War soldiers, including the young Adolf Hitler.

Adolf Hitler was wounded in the First World War. This 1916 photograph shows him (back row, second from right) during a hospital stay in the German town Beelitz.

THE STORM OF STEEL

FROM THE DIARY
OF A GERMAN STORM-TROOP OFFICER
ON THE WESTERN FRONT

ERNST JÜNGER

LIEUTENANT, 73RD HANOVERIAN FUSILIER
REGIMENT

★

With an introduction by
R. H. Mottram

The Germans had fought and defeated the French in the Franco-Prussian War of 1870-1. In so doing, they had won the provinces of Alsace and Lorraine, which became part of the new German Empire.

A **coolie** is a poorly paid worker from the Far East.

We had left lecture-room, class-room and bench behind us. We had been welded by a few weeks' training into one corporate mass inspired by the enthusiasm of one thought... to carry forward the German ideals of '70... The war was our dream of greatness, power, and glory. It was a man's work, a duel on fields whose flowers would be stained with blood.

For four long years, in torn coats and worse fed than a Chinese coolie, the German soldier was hurried from one battlefield to the next to show his iron fist yet again to a foe many times his superior in numbers, well equipped and well fed. There could be no surer sign of the might of the idea that drove us on.

THE TREATY OF VERSAILLES

The Paris Peace Conference of 1919 was largely controlled by three men: the French prime minister Georges Clemenceau, the American president Woodrow Wilson and the British prime minister David Lloyd George.

Clemenceau planned to make the Germans pay for the French lives, land and industry they had destroyed. He also intended to reduce their armed forces so that they could never start another war. Wilson had summarised his idealistic aims in a list known as the 'Fourteen Points', drawn up in January 1918. He wanted a fair treaty. The wily Lloyd George

thought that Germany should be punished, but not so harshly that it sought revenge.

Over the next six months, the precise terms of the peace treaty were hammered out. The centrepiece was Article 231, the 'War Guilt Clause', which stated that Germany was entirely to blame for the war and its results. The following articles declared that it had to pay reparations for war damage, the exact amount to be decided by a Reparation Commission. In 1921, the commission set the figure at 132 billion gold marks (£6.6 billion). Payment was to be made in the

form of ships, livestock, raw materials and other goods, as well as money.

There was more. The treaty disbanded Germany's airforce, cut its army to 100,000 men and restricted its navy to ships of a certain size. Submarines were banned. It ordered the total demilitarisation of (removal of all military forces from) the Rhineland and made Germany give some areas of land to countries such as France and Poland, others to the League of Nations (see box page 11). Further places were to hold plebiscites (votes) to decide if they wished to remain under

EUROPE AFTER THE TREATY OF VERSAILLES

League of Nations control

German territories given to other countries

Areas where people voted to remain part of Germany

Areas where people voted to join other countries

Former Austro-Hungarian Empire

Former Russian Empire

North Sea

Sweden

Baltic Sea

Latvia

Northern Schleswig

Denmark

Lithuania

Danzig

Memel: Occupied by Allies 1920-3, then seized by Lithuania

Great Britain

Southern Schleswig

East Prussia

Polish Corridor: Separates main part of Germany from East Prussia

Allenstein and Marienwerder

USSR

Netherlands

Poznan

Germany

Western Upper Silesia

Poland

Eastern Upper Silesia

Belgium

Eupen and Malmedy

Lux.

Demilitarised Rhineland: Occupied by Allied troops; no German troops allowed

Czechoslovakia

Saar coalfields placed under French rule on behalf of League of Nations

Alsace and Lorraine

Switzerland

Austria

Hungary

Romania

France

Italy

Yugoslavia

Black Sea

Bulgaria

0   300 miles

0   500km

N

The main political leaders of the Allies at the Paris Peace Conference in 1919: Lloyd George (far left), Georges Clemenceau (third from left) and Woodrow Wilson (far right) are joined by the Italian prime minister, Vittorio Orlando (second from left).

THE LEAGUE OF NATIONS

In the last of the 'Fourteen Points', Woodrow Wilson expressed his wish to establish an organisation that would promote world peace and co-operation. The first 26 Articles of the Versailles Treaty created such a body, called the League of Nations. It first met in 1920, and a year later set up the Court of International Justice to resolve international disputes. But the League was flawed. The USA chose not to become a member, while Germany was admitted only in 1926 and the USSR in 1934. Every League decision had to be unanimous, so discussions often ended in stalemate. In addition, the League had no troops to enforce the decisions that it did make, and members were often reluctant to supply them.

German control. Germany also had to abandon its colonies in Africa and the Far East. The Treaty of Versailles was signed on 28 June 1919. It was not accepted by the USA, which signed a separate treaty with Germany on 25 August 1921.

Treaties with the newly separated Austria and Hungary, whose empire had collapsed, were also part of the post-war settlement. Both countries were forced to pay reparations, had limits put on their armies and lost land (see map). Austria was forbidden to unite with Germany. More treaties dealt with other defeated powers. The Treaty of Neuilly (1919) reduced Bulgaria's land and army. The Treaty of Sèvres (1920) divided the former Ottoman (Turkish) Empire. Its Middle Eastern lands came under the control of the League of Nations.

 These are the two articles of the Treaty of Versailles (1919) that declared Germany's war guilt and demanded reparations.

Belligerency means 'being at war'.

Article 231. The Allied and Associated Governments affirm and Germany accepts the responsibility of Germany and her allies for causing all the loss and damage to which the Allied and Associated Governments and their nationals have been subjected as a consequence of the war imposed upon them by the aggression of Germany and her allies.

Article 232... The Allied and Associated Governments... require, and Germany undertakes, that she will make compensation for all damage done to the civilian population of the Allied and Associated Powers and to their property during the period of belligerency of each as an Allied or Associated Power against Germany...

THE WORLD BETWEEN THE WARS

People in Britain, France and the USA had hoped that the Treaty of Versailles would create a peaceful world where democracy flourished. However, in the 1920s and '30s, political instability and economic depression (see pages 16-17) led to the rise of both Fascism and Communism.

The Fascist movement was founded by Italian Benito Mussolini in 1919. He taught the importance of extreme nationalism – devotion to your country – and strong government, while criticising Communism and other left-wing movements. Mussolini's firm views appealed to many, and in 1922 he was able to bully the Italian king into making him prime minister (see page 13). A year later, Mussolini's armies bombarded the Greek island of Corfu. Far from supporting Greece, the weak League of Nations forced the Greeks to give in to Italian demands. In 1925, Mussolini became dictator of Italy and set about crushing all opposition to his rule.

Fascist ideals also inspired German leader Adolf Hitler (see page 16) as well as other dictators, such as Austrian Engelbert Dollfuss, who came to power during the inter-war years. The Spanish Falange Party (see box page 13) shared many Fascist views, especially a belief in nationalism. A strong nationalist movement also emerged in Japan during this era (see page 35), but it did not have one powerful leader.

After its revolution in 1917, Russia (the USSR from 1922) was ruled according to the principles of Communism. The country had only one political party, the Communist Party. Its aim, at least in theory, was to ensure that power and money were shared among the proletariat (working class), not concentrated in the hands of land and factory owners. By 1930, Joseph Stalin had become the party's leader. Communists believed that the workers in every country should join together to overthrow capitalism. The spread of Communism led to uprisings, including the Spartacist Revolt in Germany (see page 14).

Joseph Stalin (middle row second from right, in peaked cap) at a 1930 meeting of the Communist Party in Moscow. He was a ruthless dictator who killed millions of his opponents in a series of purges.

THE SPANISH CIVIL WAR

In July 1936, Francisco Franco (below right) and several other Spanish generals rebelled against the left-wing Republican government that ruled their country. The Spanish Civil War followed, lasting until March 1939. Franco's right-wing Nationalists were supported by both Hitler and Mussolini. The Republicans received assistance from Stalin – but not enough to win. After the Nationalist victory, Franco set up a military dictatorship and permitted only one political party, the Falange. The Spanish Civil War provided Germany, Italy and the USSR with a testing ground for the far larger conflict that was looming.

Victorious Nationalists enter Madrid in spring 1939 (left).

By 1922, Benito Mussolini's popularity was growing fast in Italy. In October that year he prepared his supporters (known as Blackshirts because of their uniforms) to march on the Italian capital, Rome. In order to prevent the Fascists from seizing power by force, King Victor Emmanuel III asked Mussolini to form a government. In this extract from his autobiography, Mussolini recalls the speech that he made before the marchers set off.

Italy had been on the winning side in the First World War, but afterwards it suffered serious economic failure and political conflict between left- and right-wing groups. By 1922, four governments had completely failed to solve the country's problems.

Benito Mussolini (centre) and his Blackshirts after the October 1922 March on Rome. The Blackshirts always called Mussolini *Il Duce* (the Leader).

Mussolini was a dictator. However, he did improve transport and other public services in Italy.

Fascism [marches] against a political class both cowardly and imbecile, which in four long years has not been able to give a Government to the nation. Those who form the productive class must know that Fascism wants to impose nothing more than order and discipline upon the nation and to help raise the strength which will renew progress and prosperity. The people who work in the fields and in the factories, those who work in the railroads or in the offices, have nothing to fear from the Fascist Government. Their just rights will be protected.

POST-WAR GERMANY

After the abdication of Kaiser Wilhelm II on 9 November 1918 (see page 8), Germany became a republic, and a provisional coalition government was formed. It was led by Friedrich Ebert, a member of the moderately left-wing Social Democratic Party (SPD).

Extreme left-wing groups in Germany, however, believed that the new government was not revolutionary enough. On 5 January 1919, a Communist organisation known as the Spartacist League launched a rebellion against the government in Berlin. To prevent unrest from spreading, Ebert ordered groups of ex-servicemen, called *Freikorps,* to suppress the uprising. They did so with brutal efficiency and on 15 January murdered Spartacist leaders Karl Liebknecht and Rosa Luxemburg.

This poster urged Germans to 'Vote Spartacus' – that is for the Spartacist League. By doing so, the picture suggests, they could destroy the provisional government, led by Friedrich Ebert.

On 19 January, elections were held to replace the provisional government. The SPD gained the most seats but did not have an overall majority, so it formed another coalition under Ebert. It first met in a town called Weimar because of the unrest in Berlin, so this regime became known as the Weimar Republic. The new government faced as much criticism as the old. It was blamed especially for signing the 1918 armistice and for the hated Treaty of Versailles. In 1920, the *Freikorps* briefly overthrew the government in a coup known as the Kapp *Putsch.*

In 1923, Germany fell behind with the reparation payments demanded by the Versailles Treaty. In response, French and

This illustration appeared on the cover of a French magazine in 1923. It shows French soldiers (on the right) taking control of Germany's Ruhr region. Their aim was to force the country to pay its reparations in full.

Belgian troops occupied the Ruhr, Germany's most important industrial region. Germans in the area resisted by refusing to work. As coal mines and iron foundries ground to a halt, the country's already serious economic problems worsened. The value of Germany's currency (the mark) plunged, while inflation soared.

Germany's government slowly brought the situation under control. In September 1923, the Chancellor, Gustav Stresemann, ordered the people of the Ruhr back to work. In November, financial difficulties eased when the new Rentenmark currency was introduced. (It was soon replaced by the Reichsmark.) In 1924, Stresemann, by then Foreign Minister, signed the Dawes Plan. Under the terms of this plan the USA and others loaned Germany £40 million, and reparation payments were greatly reduced.

Further improvements followed. In the 1925 Locarno treaties, Germany accepted its new western borders, abandoning its claim to Alsace, Lorraine and other territories that it had lost. As a result, it was permitted to join the League of Nations in 1926. The Young Plan of 1929 cut reparations still further and hopes for the future were high.

THE BEER HALL *PUTSCH*

Amid the chaos of 1923, the German government faced another *putsch* (revolt). It was organised by the National Socialist German Workers' (Nazi) Party, led by Adolf Hitler (see pages 16-17). On 8 November, he and 600 storm-troopers from his private army, the *Sturmabteilung* (SA), barged into a meeting at a Munich beer hall. Hitler then tried to persuade local leaders in the hall to back his attempt to seize power. At first, he seemed to win their support, but the next day police suppressed the *putsch*. Hitler was arrested and imprisoned.

Members of the *Sturmabteilung* during the *putsch* of 1923

Count Harry Kessler witnessed the ceremony on 21 August 1919 in which Friedrich Ebert (right) became the first President of the Weimar Republic. In this extract from his diaries, Kessler describes the scene.

These were black, red and gold.

The **revolution** referred to is the overthrow of the Kaiser and the establishment of the republic.

The stage was festively decorated with the new German colors and plants, gladioli and chrysanthemums...The organ played and everyone in their black jackets crowded between the plants like guests at a better-class wedding... After an organ prelude, Ebert appeared on the stage in a frock-coat, small, broad-shouldered, with gold-rimmed spectacles... Ebert spoke the words of the oath in quite a pleasing voice... the whole occasion had something touching and, above all, tragic about it. This petty drama as conclusion to the tremendous events of the war and the revolution!

THE RISE OF HITLER

In October 1929, Germany's shaky recovery came to an end. The Wall Street Crash in the USA (see box) caused worldwide economic hardship. In Germany, it paved the way for Adolf Hitler's rise to power.

The German economy was hit hard by the Great Depression. The inflation of the early 1920s returned, making savings and shares almost worthless. Unemployment rose rapidly, reaching over 8 million by 1932. To make matters worse, the USA could not afford to pay Germany the loans due under the Dawes Plan (see page 15).

The coalition government in Weimar was unable to resolve the economic crisis. So, in 1930, President Paul von Hindenburg began to rule using emergency powers granted him by the constitution, and appointed Heinrich Brüning as Chancellor. Still the situation did not improve, and in desperation many Germans turned to more extreme politicians. After the elections of September 1930, the number of Nazi Party seats in the *Reichstag* (German parliament) rose from 12 to 107.

Over the next three years, a succession of chancellors failed to end Germany's economic chaos. However the popularity of the Nazi Party, led by Hitler after his release from prison, grew steadily. In the elections of July 1932, the Nazi Party became the largest in the *Reichstag*. President von Hindenburg was wary of Nazi beliefs, but was finally persuaded to appoint Hitler as Chancellor in January 1933.

Hitler called an election for 5 March, hoping to increase further the number of Nazis in parliament. To ensure success, he ordered the SA to intimidate Communist and other opponents, and banned all press criticism of the Nazi Party. When the *Reichstag* burned down on 27 February, the fire was blamed on Communists, allowing Hitler to stir up people's fear of a left-wing revolt. But although the Nazis won 288 *Reichstag* seats, they still did not have an overall majority in parliament.

Hitler now seized control. On 23 March, the Enabling Act was passed, allowing the Nazi leader and his cabinet to make laws without the approval of parliament or president. The democratic Weimar Republic had ended. All political parties except the Nazi Party were banned.

By 1932, about half of the workforce in Germany was unemployed. People were reduced to scrabbling through rubbish dumps to look for wood or other fuel to burn on their fires, and sometimes even for food.

Adolf Hitler greets ecstatic supporters at a rally in the German city of Nuremberg, 1933. While in prison after the Beer Hall *Putsch* (see page 15), Hitler wrote a book called *Mein Kampf* (*My Struggle*) (left). It told the story of his life and outlined his ideas.

THE WALL STREET CRASH

The American economy boomed after the First World War. Factories churned out consumer goods for an eager public with money to spend. Share prices soared and investors on the Wall Street Stock Exchange in New York grew rich. But by the late 1920s, factories were producing more goods than they could sell, so profits and share prices slumped. In October 1929, thousands of investors rushed to sell shares before their value fell too steeply. But the frantic trading made prices plummet even faster. The Wall Street Crash continued until November, but the Great Depression that followed lasted for more than a decade.

Christabel Bielenberg in 1988

In 1934, a young Englishwoman called Christabel married a German lawyer and settled in Germany. In her autobiography, *The Past Is Myself* (1968), Christabel Bielenberg explains why she believed Hitler was able to seize power.

What had Hitler provided which seemed to satisfy so many and persuaded them so easily to relinquish their freedom and to turn aside from the still small voice of conscience?... Work for the unemployed, an army for the generals, a phoney religion for the gullible, a loud, insistent and not unheeded voice in international affairs for those who still smarted under the indignity of a lost war: there were also detention camps and carefully broadcast hints of what might be in store for anyone who had temerity enough to enquire into his methods too closely...

Temerity means 'boldness'.

THE ROAD TO WAR

On 2 August 1934, German president Paul von Hindenburg died. Adolf Hitler then added the duties of President to his own as Chancellor. To indicate his special role, he gave himself a new title – *Führer* (leader). Now he was fully in charge of his Nazi regime, the Third Reich.

Hitler quickly put his plans for Germany into action. He tackled unemployment at home by launching job-creation schemes such as motorway-building. At the same time, he turned his attention abroad. In *Mein Kampf* (see page 17), Hitler had stated his wish to create a Greater Germany. It was to provide *Lebensraum* (living space) for all the Germans of Europe, including those who had been under foreign rule since the Versailles Treaty.

To achieve his aims, Hitler had to overturn the Treaty of Versailles. Already in 1933, he had left the League of Nations and secretly begun to build up Germany's armed forces. He publicly rejected the disarmament clauses of Versailles and introduced conscription in 1935. Then, in 1936, he sent troops into the demilitarised Rhineland (see page 10) and established an informal alliance with Italy known as the Rome-Berlin Axis.

Britain and France responded to Hitler's actions with a policy of appeasement, as neither wanted to

This poster commemorates Germany's annexation of Austria in 1938.

provoke a war. In reply, Hitler became more daring. In March 1938 he occupied Austria, and declared its *Anschluss* (annexation). Next he demanded the return of the Sudetenland, a part of Czechoslovakia where 2.5 million Germans lived. Still anxious to keep the peace, Britain and France persuaded the Czechs to meet Hitler's demands.

After occupying the Sudetenland on 1 October 1938, Hitler had insisted that he would claim no more land. But in March 1939, his troops occupied other areas of Czechoslovakia. Britain and France now saw that appeasement was not working. They knew that Poland was another likely target for Hitler, as he wanted to retake the Polish Corridor lost at Versailles (see page 10). So they promised to guarantee Polish independence. Hitler, meanwhile,

At a conference held in Munich in 1938, British prime minister Neville Chamberlain informed Hitler that the Czechs had agreed to let Germany take over the Sudetenland. Back at home, Chamberlain proudly announced the Munich Agreement, claiming that it meant 'peace in our time'.

continued to strengthen his position. In May, Germany and Italy signed a military alliance known as the Pact of Steel, each country guaranteeing to help defend the other in case of attack. In August, Germany and the USSR signed the Nazi-Soviet Pact, agreeing not to fight each other. On 1 September, Hitler finally invaded Poland. Britain and France declared war two days later.

Sudetenland Germans welcome Nazi troops in a cover illustration from an Italian magazine, published in 1938.

THE 'NIGHT OF THE LONG KNIVES'

Hitler was prepared to do almost anything to secure his grip on power in the early 1930s. He realised that he could rule successfully only with the support of the army, whose generals despised the thuggish tactics of the SA (see page 15). So he ordered the murder of the SA leader, Ernst Röhm, and of many more SA members. The killings took place on 30 June 1934, which became known as the 'Night of the Long Knives'.

In Berlin on 26 September 1938, Hitler made a chilling speech about the Sudetenland question. This extract is taken from it.

Eduard Benes was the president of Czechoslovakia.

I desire to state before the German people that with regard to the problem of the Sudeten Germans my patience is now at an end! I have made **Mr Benes** an offer... The decision now lies in his hands: Peace or War! He will either accept this offer and now give to the Germans their freedom or we will go and fetch this freedom for ourselves... In this hour the whole German people will unite with me! It will feel my will to be its will...

Chamberlain was the British prime minister.

Eric Lomax joined the Royal Corps of Signals in May 1939. In September 1939, he was based in Edinburgh Castle, Scotland. In this extract from his autobiography, *The Railway Man* (1995), he tells what happened when war finally broke out.

In the barracks we had radios on all the time... At 11.00 am on 3rd September, we heard **Arthur Neville Chamberlain** say in his exquisite reedy voice that we were now at war with Germany. Fifteen minutes later, the air raid sirens sounded throughout Edinburgh. From Mills Mount I could look down into the main streets of the city. On Princes Street, the trams came to a standstill; every motor vehicle stopped where it was. Passengers walked with a swift nervous urgency, making for the air raid shelters... It was empty and silent now. Within minutes the streets were deserted except for the immobilized vehicles... A hand had swept over the city, stopping its heart: the war came in this silence.

WAR IN EUROPE 1939-43
THE GERMAN OFFENSIVE

Using *Blitzkrieg* tactics (speed, surprise and mobility), the Germans quickly overran much of western Poland. As Hitler and Stalin had agreed in the Nazi-Soviet Pact (see page 19), eastern Poland was invaded and occupied by the USSR. The last Polish soldiers surrendered on 5 October.

Over the following winter and in to the spring of 1940, the Allies watched for Germany to make its next move. But although there was open warfare on and under the Atlantic Ocean (see pages 24-5),

nothing stirred on land. When no further invasions occurred and no bombs fell, people began to call this era of apparent normality 'the Phoney War'.

Finally, in April 1940, Hitler launched his next offensive. He made his main target Norway for two reasons – to establish naval and air bases and to secure the sea route to Sweden, which provided Germany with vital iron ore. He planned to occupy Denmark at the same time. German troops poured in to both countries on 9 April. The Danes

GERMAN CAMPAIGNS 1938-40

German invasion April 1940

German invasion May-June 1940

| 0 | 300 miles |
| 0 | 500km |

Becomes puppet state under German control 1939

Slovak territory seized by Hungary 1939

Seized by Germany
1938
March 1939
September 1939
Seized by USSR
1939 and 1940

surrendered almost at once in the face of this unexpected attack. The Norwegians, with British and French support, held out until mid-June.

By this time another German offensive, codenamed *Fall Gelb* (Case Yellow), was under way. It began on 10 May with the air bombardment of Belgium and the Netherlands. Paratroopers then landed and ground forces invaded. The Belgians were forced to retreat and the Dutch to surrender on 14 May. The French army and the British Expeditionary Force advanced east to meet the enemy.

Next, the Germans began their drive into France. The bulk of the army invaded through the Ardennes region of Belgium, avoiding the Maginot Line where many defending French troops were based. The Germans then advanced rapidly while the Allies retreated to the Channel coast. On 26 May, Operation Dynamo, the evacuation of British, French

Germans seize Kastrup airport in Copenhagen, the capital of Denmark, in April 1940. The country was occupied for the next five years.

and Belgian troops from the beaches of Dunkirk, began. In 10 days, hundreds of boats ferried about 340,000 soldiers across the English Channel to safety.

The Battle of France continued as the German army powered its way south. Paris fell on 14 June and an armistice was signed eight days later. The Germans occupied northern France and governed it directly. Marshal Philippe Pétain was allowed to set up a separate government in Vichy to rule the south, but only under German control.

By the end of the war, Bernard Montgomery was a field marshal in the British army (see page 57). But at the time of Dunkirk, he was a divisional commander. In his memoirs, published in 1958, he describes his experiences during the evacuation.

The ships that rescued the Allied soldiers at Dunkirk varied from navy destroyers to small civilian craft. Many could not come right up to the beaches, so piers were built out into the sea.

A.D.C. is short for 'aide-de-camp', a junior officer who works as the assistant of a senior officer.

I ordered that any men who could not be embarked from the beaches were to move along the beach to Dunkirk and get on board ships in the harbour. The next night [the] situation on the beaches was not good, for some of the improvised piers we had made began to break up; many had to walk to Dunkirk. While standing on the beach, my A.D.C. was wounded in the head by a splinter of shell. I cursed him soundly for not wearing his steel helmet, quite forgetting that I was not wearing one myself – as he pointed out!...

OPERATION SEALION

Hitler had seized France with comparative ease. Next he began to look further afield. On 16 July 1940 he issued *Führer* Directive 16, which called for the invasion of Britain. The codename for the plan was *Seelöwe* (Sealion).

In this task, Hitler faced a formidable new opponent: Winston Churchill. Churchill had become British prime minister in May 1940 after Neville Chamberlain resigned. In the following weeks, with a combination of stirring speeches (see document page 23) and practical preparations, he roused the British people to combat the expected Nazi offensive. On 10 July, the *Luftwaffe* began to bomb towns and shipping along England's south coast. The Battle of Britain was under way.

The Germans' aim was to seize control of British air space so that their ships could cross the Channel in safety. From 13 August, they bombed Royal Air Force bases and radar stations. The *Luftwaffe* made steady progress, but Hitler wanted quick results so that the invasion could begin before winter set in. So he ordered the *Luftwaffe* to attack a new target: London.

The intensive air raids on London, known as the Blitz, began in early September 1940. The sound of German bombers and the sight of fighter planes – German Messerschmitts, British Spitfires and Hurricanes – engaged in aerial combat became regular features of life in the city. However the *Luftwaffe* was unable to inflict a swift defeat on the RAF, so *Seelöwe* was called off on 17 September.

LOSING THE BATTLE

In the Battle of Britain, approximately 2500 *Luftwaffe* aircraft were pitted against just 1000 RAF planes. Many *Luftwaffe* pilots were experienced, having fought in the Spanish Civil War (see page 13), while the RAF had a serious shortage of trained fliers. However, the *Luftwaffe* faced other major problems that led to its failure. Its aeroplanes could not travel far without returning to base for refuelling, nor could they carry many bombs. In addition, their incoming flights were detected by Chain Home (CH), a network of 50 radar stations that had been positioned along the British coast in 1937. As a result, RAF fighter planes knew exactly where to intercept the invaders.

A painting of a Chain Home radar station

The scene after a *Luftwaffe* bombing raid over London. During the Blitz, some 40,000 people were killed and many buildings were damaged beyond repair.

British prime minister Winston Churchill visits anti-aircraft guns and their operators in London. His distinctive figure, wearing a bow tie and smoking a large cigar, became a symbol of resistance to the Nazi threat.

Winston Churchill knew how to engage the hearts and minds of the British people for the fight against Germany. In this speech, made on 18 June 1940, he rallied people for the crucial task ahead.

The Battle of Britain continued into October, when Germany was forced to abandon its plan to destroy British air power.

The *Luftwaffe* remained active in Britain's skies for many more months, however. The Blitz bombing of London was extended to other cities such as Coventry, where the cathedral was all but destroyed in an attack on 14 November 1940. Germany's aim now was to undermine morale as well as to wipe out military bases and factories. But the British public responded with a spirit of determined endurance. The Blitz lasted until May 1941. By that time, the *Luftwaffe* had dropped 35,000 tonnes of bombs on Britain, 19,000 of them on London.

...the Battle of France is over. I expect that the Battle of Britain is about to begin... The whole fury and might of the enemy must very soon be turned on us. Hitler knows that he will have to break us in this island or lose the war. If we can stand up to him, all Europe may be free and the life of the world may move forward into broad, sunlit uplands... Let us therefore brace ourselves to our duties and so bear ourselves that, if the British Empire and its Commonwealth last for a thousand years, men will still say, 'This was their finest hour.'

The day-to-day experience of the Blitz was less uplifting, as this letter indicates. It was written by Doll Ratcliff, who worked in London, to her husband Jack, an army captain.

A.R.P. stands for 'Air Raid Precautions'. A.R.P. wardens had various duties, including enforcement of the black-out. This was the covering of windows and doors with thick curtains at night so that lights inside could not guide enemy aircraft to their targets.

15 Clarges Street
W.1.
Sept. 10th.

My dear Jack,
The last three nights have been absolute hell! We are bombed from about 8.30 p.m. to 5.30 a.m. every night and I have not had more than 2 or 3 hours sleep on either night. I sleep in the afternoon whenever I can but I would just give anything for a quiet night in the country... Everyone is tired out, they say the firemen, A.R.P. and ambulance drivers are beyond praise. The hospitals are packed with casualties and the damage all along the river has been very great...

THE BATTLE OF THE ATLANTIC

As a small island nation, Britain was dependent on food, fuel and raw materials brought by ship from abroad. German warships and U-boats set out to prevent such supplies reaching British shores as soon as the Second World War began. The Atlantic Ocean became a battle zone.

From 1939, merchant ships sailed in convoys with navy escorts to minimise the danger from U-boats. Accompanying warships were fitted with Asdic, a submarine-detecting sonar system. Despite these measures, Admiral Karl Dönitz's fleet of 57 U-boats sank 114 Allied ships in the first year of the war.

After the fall of Norway and France (see pages 20-1), the Battle of the Atlantic moved up a gear. Now German shipping could operate from more ports over a wider area. U-boats began to attack in 'wolf pack' groups, and to receive support from aircraft, which bombed and spied on enemy ships. By 1941, U-boat numbers were increasing by about 20 per month and Allied shipping losses were growing ominously high.

Britain fought back with more air support and better-equipped escort ships for convoys. Intelligence (see box page 25) helped shipping avoid U-boats altogether. Assistance came from the USA, too. In March 1941 it passed the Lend-Lease Act,

A German U-boat. 'U-boat' is a short English form of the German word *Unterseeboot* meaning 'undersea boat' (submarine).

which arranged for the loan of money and equipment to the Allies. Many ships were provided as part of the deal. The US Navy also began to escort shipping in the Western Atlantic.

After the USA joined the war in December 1941 (see page 37), many of its warships were sent to the Pacific Ocean. However, no convoy system operated along the American east coast at first, so merchant ships there were an easy target for U-boats. In the first six months of 1942, the Germans sank 492 vessels in the region.

By 1943 the balance of power at sea had turned against Germany, for many reasons. Improved radar helped vessels to detect and avoid U-boats before they struck. Support groups of escort ships rushed to assist

The Royal Navy sank the *Bismarck,* one of Germany's biggest battleships, in the Atlantic in May 1941.

convoys that were under attack. Aircraft carriers accompanied convoys to give on-the-spot air support. American B-24 Liberator bombers were able to strike in sea areas once out of range, and mass-produced American cargo vessels called Liberty ships replaced merchant vessels faster than U-boats could sink them.

By mid-1943, Dönitz realised that U-boats would not be able to win the war by depriving Britain of food and other vital supplies. But his submarines continued to harass Allied vessels throughout the war, and even in 1945 sank almost 300,000 tonnes of enemy shipping.

Admiral Dönitz published his memoirs, *Zehn Jahre und Zwanzig Tage (Ten Years and Twenty Days)*, in 1958. In this extract, he reproduces a captain's report about a U-boat attack off the Atlantic coast of Africa.

On the beam means 'to the side'.

Admiral Karl Dönitz is at the centre of this photograph (with the most stripes on his sleeves), surrounded by some of the naval officers who served under him.

CRACKING THE CODES

While ships and U-boats fought battles at sea, British and German intelligence experts engaged in mental duels. One aim of the British Ultra intelligence unit was to intercept and decode messages containing information about U-boat routes. Its German counterpart, the B-Dienst, tried to discover convoy positions. The Royal Navy code was relatively easy to crack and allowed U-boats to target convoys with some accuracy. The Germans' Enigma code proved more resistant, but progress was made from May 1941 when an encoding machine was found in a sunken U-boat. The German navy code was fully broken in 1942, making it possible to divert Atlantic convoys out of harm's way.

One of the Enigma machines used by the Germans to put secret messages into code

2100 means '9 p.m.'.

April 30 [1942]. 2100... Found a convoy consisting of some fourteen large, fully-laden ships of between 5,000 and 7,000 tons with an escort of three destroyers and five other escort vessels. Stood off in darkness and a squall of rain... As the escort ahead and on the beam was strong, penetrated into the convoy from astern. Night dark with occasional sheet lightning. Fired six independent torpedoes, depth 15 feet, targets, five freighters and one tanker. All six hit amidships... Dived to 500 feet... Loud noise of sinking ships.

Astern means 'from the back'.

WAR IN NORTH AFRICA

Despite its alliance with Germany (see page 19), Italy did not declare war on the Allies until 10 June 1940. The unimpressive efforts of its army contributed nothing to the fall of France. Benito Mussolini (see pages 12-13) then decided that the time had come to make his mark.

Mussolini had long dreamed of creating a 20th-century Roman Empire. When he came to power in 1922, Italy already had several African colonies, including Libya. In 1935, Mussolini occupied Abyssinia (present-day Ethiopia). After declaring war on the Allies, he set his sights on British-controlled Egypt and its vital shipping link, the Suez Canal.

The Italians invaded Egypt from Libya in September 1940. There were about 250,000 Italian troops, while General Sir Archibald Wavell led only 31,000 British soldiers. However, the Italians were forced to retreat after advancing just 80km. British infantry and tanks stormed after them into Libya.

In February 1941, Hitler sent the Afrika Korps, under the command of Lieutenant General Erwin Rommel, to the aid of the Italians. In March, Rommel mounted a counter-attack, forcing the British back towards Egypt. But although he besieged the Libyan fortress of Tobruk, he was unable to seize it from the defending Australian troops.

In July 1941, Wavell was replaced by General Sir Claude Auchinleck. He launched Operation Crusader, an attempt to end the Tobruk siege and retake eastern Libya, in November. Tobruk was relieved in December and Rommel forced west.

The commanding figure standing in the front of this battle-scarred jeep is Lieutenant General, later Field Marshal, Erwin Rommel. His exploits in North Africa earned him the nickname 'the Desert Fox'.

NORTH AFRICA 1942-3

British troops at El Alamein in October 1942. The troops' commander, General Bernard Montgomery, predicted that the fighting there would be 'one of the decisive battles of history'. He was quickly proved right.

The Germans struck back in January 1942. In June, Tobruk was recaptured and the British fell back to El Alamein in Egypt.

In August 1942, General Sir Harold Alexander replaced Auchinleck, and General Bernard Montgomery took direct charge of the British 8th Army. Montgomery was supplied with more aircraft, tanks and troops, and soon led 230,000 men. On 23 October, he attacked at El Alamein. Rommel retreated 12 days later. The Allies had won their first major victory of the war against the Germans and Italians.

On 8 November, the Allies began Operation Torch, landing American and British troops under US general Dwight D. Eisenhower in Morocco and Algeria. By early 1943, they were fighting Rommel's retreating troops, as well as German reinforcements, in Tunisia. Meanwhile Montgomery, having taken Tripoli in January, was attacking from the east. Hitler now realised that North Africa was lost and ordered Rommel home in March. Tunis fell to the Allies on 7 May, and on 13 May the Axis Powers in Africa surrendered.

EAST AFRICAN ENCOUNTERS

Britain and Italy also clashed in East Africa. In July 1940, troops based in the Italian colonies of Abyssinia, Eritrea and Italian Somaliland briefly crossed the border into the British colonies of Sudan and Kenya. In August, they occupied British Somaliland. The British quickly built up their forces in the region, then struck back. Italian Somaliland fell in February and British Somaliland was recaptured in March. Eritrea and Abyssinia were both taken in April. The Abyssinian emperor, Haile Selassie, returned to power from exile on 5 May.

Keith Douglas served as leader of a British tank crew in North Africa and wrote a book and some poetry about his experiences. This extract comes from one poem, *Vergissmeinnicht*, in which the writer describes finding a dead German soldier in the desert.

Gunpit spoil means the earth dug up to create a placement for a gun.

This is German for 'Steffi: do not forget me'.

Three weeks gone and the combatants gone
returning over the nightmare ground
we found the place again, and found
the soldier sprawling in the sun.

...

Look. Here in the gunpit spoil
the dishonoured picture of his girl
who has put: Steffi. Vergissmeinnicht
in a copybook gothic script.

...

But she would weep to see today
how on his skin the swart flies move;
the dust upon the paper eye
and the burst stomach like a cave.

WAR IN THE BALKANS

Mussolini also had plans for expansion into the large area of south-eastern Europe known as the Balkans. Already in April 1939, before the war began, Italian troops had occupied the Balkan state of Albania. As a result, Britain had promised to guarantee the independence of Greece and Romania if they were attacked. But Mussolini was undeterred. On 28 October 1940, he launched a campaign from Albania into Greece.

Italy's armies fared as badly in the mountains of Greece as they had in the deserts of Egypt. By December, the Greeks had forced them far back into

Albania. The Greek ruler, Ioannis Metaxas, rejected Britain's offers of ground troops, both because he felt that they were unnecessary and because he feared that British involvement might tempt the Germans to invade, too. But Metaxas died on 29 January 1941, and by early March, British troops from North Africa were arriving in Greece.

Hitler, meanwhile, was making his own plans for the Balkans. Originally, there were two main reasons for his interest in the region. First, he wanted to secure the area before his invasion of the USSR (see pages 30-1), which stands on the

Balkans' eastern border. Second, he wanted to protect the vast oilfields in Ploesti, Romania, which fuelled Germany's war machine. Italy's plight and Britain's arrival in the Balkans made a German invasion appear even more essential.

While planning his attack on Greece, codenamed Operation Marita, Hitler won the support of other Balkan states by negotiation. Romania had already joined the Tripartite Pact, whose original members were Germany, Italy and Japan (see page 36). Bulgaria and Yugoslavia joined the Pact in March 1941. But there was a coup in Yugoslavia on 27 March and its new government rejected the agreement. Hitler decided that Yugoslavia as well as Greece would have to be occupied and brought under direct Nazi rule.

Hitler began his Balkan offensive on 6 April. Yugoslavia was soon completely overwhelmed, falling to the Germans on 17 April. Greece held out a little longer – the defending Greek troops were forced to surrender on 23 April. By 30 April the British forces, under constant bombardment from the *Luftwaffe*, had completed a sea evacuation to Crete (see box page 29). *Blitzkrieg* tactics had triumphed once more.

Italian soldiers invading Greece in 1940. Much of the fighting took place in mountain areas, where they were no match for the local Greeks.

CRETAN COLLAPSE

Britain occupied Crete in October 1940. After the evacuation from Greece in April 1941, the island's commander, Major-General Bernard Freyberg, prepared for a German invasion. The Ultra intelligence unit (see page 25) gave him detailed information about General Kurt Student's plan of attack. So when aerial bombardment and paratroop landings began on 20 May, his forces were ready to fight. But despite staunch defence by New Zealand troops, the airfield at Máleme soon fell. German reinforcements then flew in, and from late May the British had to evacuate again. About 12,000 men were left behind and taken prisoner.

The remains of an RAF aircraft that crashed during the battle for Crete

German soldiers gaze up at the Nazi flag on the Acropolis. The flag was red with a white circle containing a black swastika in the centre.

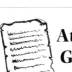 **Athens, the Greek capital, fell to the Germans on 27 April 1941. German archaeologist Walter Wrede was head of the Nazi Party in the city at that time. In this extract from the 1942 *Jahrbuch des Auslands-Organisation der NSDAP (Year Book of the Nazi Party's Overseas Organisation)*, he recalls one of the momentous events of that day.**

The **Acropolis** is the high, central area of Athens where the ancient temple of the Parthenon stands.

A **belvedere** is any building from which there is a good view.

A police official comes to the door at 9.30 and tells us that German troops are making their way to the Acropolis. There they will hoist the German flag. I spring to our lookout post on the upper floor. Correct! From the mast of the Belvedere of the city shines the red of the Reich's flag! The cry: 'Swastika over the Acropolis!' rings through the house. In a few minutes we are all gathered together to give thanks to the Führer. The national anthem carries through the now open windows into the streets outside... Flowers and cigarettes are quickly found, and thus prepared we stand at the windows waiting for the first German soldiers.

The **flowers and cigarettes** were to be thrown at the German soldiers as a sign of welcome.

OPERATION BARBAROSSA

In 1939, Hitler and Stalin had signed the Nazi-Soviet Pact (see page 19). However, for Hitler this was only an alliance of convenience. He hated the Communist ideals of the USSR, and thought that its Slav people were *Untermenschen* – subhumans (see page 46). He also coveted the USSR's land, which he wanted as *Lebensraum* for Germans.

The alliance continued into 1940, but tensions between the two partners increased. Hitler believed that the USSR was a threat to Germany's interests in the Balkans and Scandinavia, and he began to make plans for an invasion. In November, when Stalin resisted joining Germany, Italy and Japan in the Tripartite Pact (see page 36), Hitler decided to act. He issued *Führer* Directive 21, codenamed Operation Barbarossa, in December. By mid-1941, after securing the Balkans, he was ready to invade the USSR.

The Germans launched their offensive on 22 June 1941. It was the largest ground attack ever seen, involving 3.5 million men. German forces were divided into three. Army Group North headed for Leningrad, Army Group Centre for Moscow, and Army Group South for Kiev. Stalin was taken completely by surprise. His Red Army was unprepared and equipped with outdated tanks and weapons.

The Germans hoped to encircle and destroy their enemies quickly. But although

THE INVASION OF THE USSR

the Panzer tank divisions made fast progress, the offensive faced major problems. The infantry could not keep up with the tank advance, many tanks broke down and could not be replaced, and summer rains turned the roads into impassable swamps. Red Army resistance remained fierce, despite severe losses. The army was also able to renew itself by mobilising more of the USSR's vast population.

By mid-August, Army Group South had captured Kiev. Army Group North reached Leningrad in September and began a bitter siege that lasted until 1944. Army Group Centre began to advance on Moscow in October, but its men were exhausted and

supplies were slow to reach them from the distant border. Soon the brutal Russian winter stopped them in their tracks. Without suitable cold-weather clothing, thousands of men developed frostbite, while the oil froze in their cars and tanks.

The Red Army, however, was used to the icy conditions. On 6 December, led by new commander General (later Marshal) Georgi Zhukov, the Soviets were able to launch a Moscow counter-offensive. Hitler ordered his men not to retreat at any cost, but they were forced back. The Soviet capital had been spared, and by spring 1942 there was still everything to fight for.

The German advance into the USSR was swift and without mercy. Soldiers sometimes burned villages before continuing on their way.

In this diary extract, a German soldier describes the terrible conditions that he and his comrades endured as they marched towards Moscow in the autumn of 1941.

Even in September and before the advent of winter, there was incessant rain and a cold north-east wind, so that every night there was a scramble for shelter, squalid and bug-ridden though it usually was. When this could not be found, the troops plumbed the very depths of wretchedness. The rain, cold and lack of rest increased sickness that, in normal circumstances, would have warranted admission to hospital; but the sick had to march in the column over distances of up to **twenty-five miles a day**, since there was no transport to carry them and they could not be left behind in the bandit-infested forest. The regulation boots... were falling to pieces. All ranks were filthy and bearded, with dirty, rotting and verminous underclothing; typhus was shortly to follow.

Twenty-five miles is equal to 40km.

MOVING EAST

Many of the factories that produced tanks, guns, ammunition and other Soviet war equipment were based in and around Leningrad and Kiev, as well as on the western fringes of Moscow. As the German armies advanced, they seized as many of these vital plants as they could. To preserve the remainder, Soviet engineers dismantled them, then transported them east by rail in a massive industrial evacuation. More than 1500 factories were uprooted in this way, and by autumn 1941, about 80 per cent of the USSR's military industry was heading east.

While Soviet men fought on the front lines, many Soviet women made weapons and ammunition to help in the struggle against Germany.

STALINGRAD

Once the springtime thaw of 1942 had passed, the thoughts of both Hitler and Stalin turned again to winning the struggle for the USSR. The Germans struck first in early May, overrunning much of the Crimea (see map page 30). However, Hitler's key aim now was to capture the industry and oilfields of the Caucasus, which supplied the Red Army.

Hitler launched the main offensive into the Caucasus on 28 June. The Germans made good progress, partly because Stalin had expected an attack on Moscow, so had concentrated his troops there. Then, in mid-July, Hitler divided his forces. Army Group A was ordered to continue south, while Army Group B was sent east towards Stalingrad, an important city on the Volga River. In a separate development, the city of Sevastopol had already fallen to Hitler's forces on 3 July, leaving the whole Crimea under German control.

The German attack on Stalingrad began on 19 August. Over the following weeks, the *Luftwaffe* supported the troops and artillery on the ground with heavy bombing. By September, the German Sixth Army under General Friedrich von Paulus was making its way through the city's burning ruins. It met fierce resistance from Red Army troops. Each house and factory was defended to the death in hand-to-hand fighting. But by November, when the winter cold was biting deep, much of the city was in the hands of the Germans.

Then came the daring Soviet counter-stroke, Operation Uranus, devised by Marshal Zhukov (see page 30) and Marshal Aleksandr Vasilevsky. On 19 November, troops attacked not the strong German forces inside Stalingrad, but the weaker Romanians and Italians to the north and south. Tanks smashed through their shocked ranks and within four days the Soviets had encircled the city. A rescue attempt failed, and the *Luftwaffe* could not fly in enough supplies. Soon the 300,000 Germans trapped in Stalingrad began to starve.

Worse was to come for Hitler, as more Soviet gains threatened Army Group A in the Caucasus.

Soldiers fought to the death for almost every building in Stalingrad. The Germans were determined to seize 'Stalin's city'. The Soviets were equally determined not to let them do so.

The Nazi leader was concerned that the escape route via Rostov would soon be cut off, so authorised the army's withdrawal in December. He refused, however, to allow the Germans in Stalingrad to abandon the fight. But after suffering more losses in a new Soviet attack, General von Paulus surrendered on 31 January 1943. German dreams of victory in the USSR had received a crushing blow.

Flares light up the night sky above the Kursk battleground, set off by Soviet troops to guide their tanks to German targets.

The following extracts are taken from the diary of a German Sixth Army soldier. It was found in the ruins of Stalingrad.

Field Marshal Eric von Manstein secured the Crimea for Germany in July 1942 before attempting the relief of Stalingrad.

THE BATTLE OF KURSK

After Stalingrad, the Soviets continued to push west. But Hitler was not yet defeated. In March 1943, his forces staged a successful counter-attack in the Ukraine. Next they planned to assault Kursk, where Soviet troops were exposed in a front-line salient (bulge). However, Hitler delayed the offensive until the summer, during which time the Soviets learned of his plan and strengthened their defences with mines and artillery. When the German tanks moved in on 5 July, they met this deadly opposition. Still they persisted until, on 12 July, the Soviets counter-attacked. The greatest tank battle in history followed, with about 700 German vehicles ranged against about 900 from the Soviet army. This brutal armoured clash led Hitler to call off his offensive the next day. From then on, the Soviet advance was unstoppable.

November 29. We are encircled. It was announced this morning that the Führer had said: 'The army can trust me to do everything necessary to ensure supplies and rapidly break the [Soviet] encirclement.'

December 3. We are on hunger rations and waiting for the rescue that the Führer promised...

December 7. Rations have been cut to such an extent that the soldiers are suffering terribly from hunger; they are issuing one loaf of stale bread for five men...

December 18. The officers today told the soldiers to be prepared for action. General Manstein is approaching Stalingrad from the south with strong forces. This brought hope to the soldiers' hearts. God, let it be!...

December 25. The Russian radio has announced the defeat of Manstein. Ahead of us is either death or captivity.

December 26. The horses have already been eaten. I would eat a cat... The soldiers look like corpses or lunatics, looking for something to put in their mouths. They no longer take cover from Russian shells; they haven't the strength to walk, run away and hide. A curse on this war!

CHAPTER 3

WAR IN THE PACIFIC 1941-3
THE RISE OF JAPAN

In the late 19th century, Japan began a process of rapid modernisation. It did not have enough of its own raw materials, for example iron ore and oil, to use in its new factories. So it started a period of aggressive expansion on the Asian mainland.

Japan built up its empire gradually. In 1904-5, it defeated the Russians, forcing them out of Manchuria in northern China, and stationing troops to guard the South Manchurian Railway. By 1910, it had occupied Korea. During the First World War, Japan fought on the side of the Allies and took over more lands in China. After the war, it made plans to increase its territories in China, as civil war had weakened Chinese resistance. But by then the USA

and Britain were on the alert, fearful of the Japanese threat to their own Pacific interests.

The growth of Japan's navy was of particular concern to Western powers. In 1921, the USA hosted the Washington Conference to discuss this and associated issues. Three treaties resulted. In the naval armament treaty, all participants agreed to limit their navies. Japan also agreed that its navy would remain smaller than those of the USA and Britain. In the Four-Power Treaty, delegates from four nations agreed not to threaten each other's possessions in the region. In the Nine-Power Treaty, nine nations pledged to continue a policy that gave all countries equal trading rights with China.

JAPANESE AND US TERRITORIES IN THE PACIFIC

The busy scene at the 1921 Washington Conference

SPREADING SOUTH

Once they had invaded China in 1937, the Japanese advanced quickly. After Beijing had fallen, they moved south to the coastal city of Shanghai. There they clashed with forces led by Chiang Kai-shek, head of China's Nationalist government. Japan took the city in November, after 40,000 of its soldiers and 270,000 Chinese troops had died in the fighting. Nanjing, then China's capital, was occupied in December, so the government fled to Hankow. When the city fell in October 1938, the Nationalists moved to Chungking, which became their wartime capital. By that time, a vast swathe of land along China's east coast was under Japanese control.

Japan was badly affected by the Wall Street Crash of 1929 (see page 17). During the Depression that followed, the nation's military leaders became increasingly powerful. They believed that further expansion overseas would ease the country's economic problems and forced the government to act. In 1931, Japanese troops invaded and occupied all of Manchuria, renaming the region Manchukuo. The League of Nations took no real action against the Japanese, but it did publish a report that found them guilty of wrong-doing. As a result, Japan left the League in 1933.

Tension increased as the years passed. In 1935, Japan announced that it no longer accepted the Washington Conference limitations on its navy. In 1936, it signed a co-operation treaty with Germany. Then, in July 1937, it used a clash between Chinese and Japanese troops outside Beijing as an excuse for a full-scale invasion of China. Some historians think that this event, not the Pearl Harbor attack (see page 37), marks the true beginning of the Second World War in the Pacific.

The following extract is taken from the Four-Power Treaty signed at the Washington Conference on 13 December 1921 (see page 34).

The High Contracting Parties means 'the governments who have signed the treaty': the USA, Britain, France and Japan.

The treaty was weak because it did not define precisely how it was to be enforced.

Article I. The High Contracting Parties agree as between themselves to respect their rights in relation to their insular possessions and insular dominions in the region of the Pacific Ocean.

If there should develop between any of the High Contracting Parties a controversy arising out of any Pacific question and involving their said rights which is not satisfactorily settled by diplomacy and is likely to affect the harmonious accord now happily subsisting between them, they shall invite the other High Contracting Parties to a joint conference to which the whole subject will be referred for consideration and adjustment.

PEARL HARBOR AND AFTER

THE WAR IN THE PACIFIC

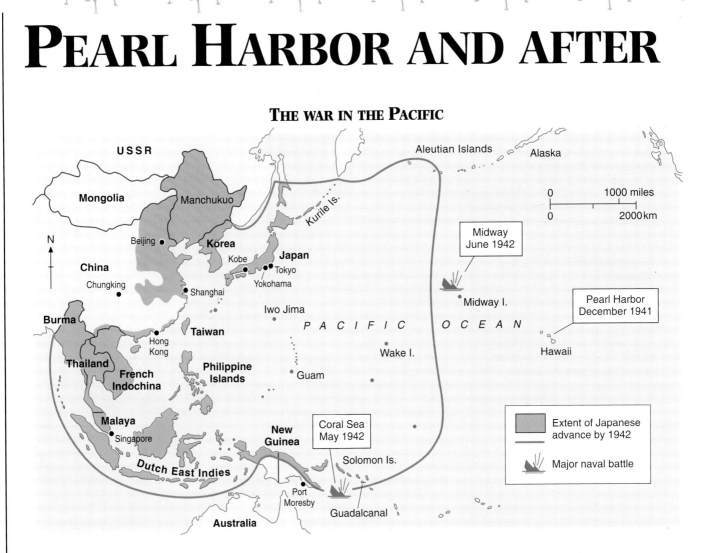

After its success in China, Japan's ambitions grew. In November 1938, it announced its plans for Southeast Asia. Western powers, such as Britain, France, the Netherlands and the USA, were to be expelled from their colonies in the region. The same lands, with their rich resources of rubber, tin and oil, would become part of a new, Japanese-controlled Greater East Asia Co-Prosperity Sphere.

The situation in Europe soon played into Japan's hands. By 1940, France and the Netherlands were under German control and Britain was busy resisting the Nazi threat. As a result, the Southeast Asian colonies of all three nations were vulnerable to attack. US President Franklin D. Roosevelt realised that new problems were looming so he looked for ways to force a Japanese withdrawal from China, and to protect both American and European territories in the Pacific.

Roosevelt decided to stop Japan's empire-building by imposing economic sanctions. In July 1940, he placed strict limits on the sale of iron and

oil to Japan. This was a serious blow, as Japan was heavily dependent on American imports. But it refused to back down. In September 1940, Japanese forces occupied parts of Indochina, a French colony.

Japan now prepared itself for a possible war in the Pacific. Later in September, it signed the Tripartite Pact with Germany and Italy. Then, in April 1941, it agreed a neutrality pact with Stalin so that it could concentrate on its plans for Southeast Asia without fear of aggression from the USSR. The USA tried to resolve the situation by extending sanctions and holding talks with the Japanese. Neither measure worked.

In July 1941, tension mounted still further when Japan formally annexed the whole of Indochina. In response, Roosevelt ended all trade with the Japanese and denied them access to all money and possessions held in the USA. In October, General Hideki Tojo became Japanese prime minister and sent a special ambassador to the USA for discussions. However, American insistence that Japan completely evacuate both China and Indochina was unacceptable. By November there was stalemate.

The stalemate ended early on 7 December 1941 when Japanese bombers attacked the American fleet at Pearl Harbor in Hawaii. The base was taken completely by surprise – eight battleships were sunk or badly damaged and more than 2400 sailors killed. On 8 December, the USA declared war on Japan. On 11 December, Germany and Italy declared war on the USA. The Second World War had turned into a truly global conflict.

EXTENDING THE EMPIRE

After Pearl Harbor, Japan struck many other Pacific targets. Of the American-controlled territories, Wake Island and Guam fell in December, while the Philippines held out until spring 1942, thanks to a fierce defence led by General Douglas MacArthur. Britain lost Hong Kong on Christmas Day 1941, retreated from Malaya in January 1942, surrendered Singapore in February and left Burma in May. The Dutch East Indies (now Indonesia) also became part of Japan's empire in 1942.

Smoke and flames engulf American warships in Pearl Harbor after the Japanese attack.

During the 1980s, American writer Studs Terkel travelled the USA interviewing people about their experiences during the Second World War. He published their reminiscences in *"The Good War"* (1985), from which this extract is taken. The speaker was John Garcia, a Hawaiian.

West Virginia was the name of a US Navy battleship.

I was sixteen years old, employed as a pipe fitter apprentice at Pearl Harbor Navy Yard. On December 7, 1941, oh, around 8: A.M., my grandmother woke me. She informed me that the Japanese were bombing Pearl Harbor. I said, "They're just practicing." She said, no, it was real and the announcer is requesting that all Pearl Harbor workers report to work. I went out on the porch and I could see the anti-aircraft fire up in the sky... I was asked by [an] officer to go into the water and get sailors out that had been blown off the ships. Some were unconscious, some were dead. I brought out I don't know how many bodies... The following morning, I went with my tools to the West Virginia. It had turned turtle, totally upside down... We spent about a month cutting the superstructure... tilting it back on its hull. About three hundred men we cut out of there were still alive by the eighteenth day.

THE AMERICAN FIGHTBACK

Japan's advance into American-controlled Pacific territories had been both swift and shocking. By the middle of 1942, the USA was urgently considering how to regain its lost territory. The Japanese were in a dilemma, too. Some military leaders wanted simply to defend their large new empire, while others hoped to increase their lands still further.

Japan finally decided to capture New Guinea, which would give it access to Australia. In May 1942, it prepared to invade Port Moresby, the island's capital. But Magic, the American intelligence operation, had cracked the Japanese naval codes and Admiral Chester Nimitz, now Commander-in-Chief of the US Pacific Fleet, knew about the attack in advance. He sent a naval task force, including aircraft carriers USS *Lexington* and USS *Yorktown*, to the region. In the Battle of the Coral Sea on 7-8 May, the *Lexington* was lost. But Japan abandoned the New Guinea invasion after one of its carriers was sunk and another damaged.

Admiral Isoroku Yamamoto, Commander-in-Chief of the Japanese Combined Fleet, then moved to tackle the USA head-on by attacking the American island of Midway in the Central Pacific. In so doing, he hoped to tempt the remainder of the US Pacific Fleet out of Pearl Harbor and destroy it in mid-ocean. Again, Magic forewarned Admiral Nimitz of the offensive, and again he sent a task force to stop the Japanese in their tracks. By June 1942, Yamamoto had 145 ships in the Midway area, Nimitz a mere 50. But the USA had more aircraft, based on carriers and on Midway itself, and they were to prove decisive.

The Battle of Midway began on 4 June 1942 when bombers from Yamamoto's four main aircraft carriers raided the island. After Midway-based American bombers struck back, the admiral ordered a second raid. Meanwhile, carrier-based bombers from Nimitz's fleet had set out for the Japanese ships. They arrived as the second wave of

During the Battle of Midway, the Americans lost one aircraft carrier, USS *Yorktown*. It was sunk by a Japanese submarine on 6 June 1942.

THE DOOLITTLE RAID

Many American people wanted to avenge Pearl Harbor quickly. So in April 1942 the government permitted Major-General James Doolittle to launch an air attack on Japan itself. The method used was risky. First the aircraft carrier USS *Hornet* moved as close to Japan as it dared. Then long-range B-25 bombers took off from its deck and headed for Tokyo, Yokohama, Kobe and other cities. Many bombs hit their targets and 71 of the 80 airmen involved returned from their mission safely. The Japanese assumed that the Doolittle Raid came from the Midway area. This was one of the reasons they decided to attack the island in 1942.

Yamamoto's bombers, just back from Midway, were refuelling and reloading torpedoes on deck. Many American planes were shot down. But enough dive-bombers hit their targets to send three Japanese carriers up in flames. The fourth was hit some hours later.

The American victory at Midway turned the tide of the Pacific War, allowing the USA to go on the offensive. Its first move was in August 1942 against Japanese troops constructing an airfield on Guadalcanal, one of the Solomon Islands. The Japanese withdrew after six months of intense fighting. The long American recovery had finally begun.

Commander Mitsuo Fuchida led the air attack on Pearl Harbor. During the Battle of Midway, he served on the aircraft carrier *Akagi*. Here he describes the terrifying moment when American dive-bombers began the descent that destroyed the ship. Fuchida was wounded in the raid, but survived to fight again. He became an American citizen in 1966.

Five minutes! Who would have dreamed that the tide of battle would shift completely in that brief interval? Visibility was good. Clouds were gathering at about three thousand meters, however, and though there were occasional breaks, they afforded good concealment for approaching enemy planes. At 10.24 the order to start launching came from the bridge by voice-tube. The air officer flapped a white flag, and the first Zero fighter gathered speed and whizzed off the deck. At that instant a look-out screamed: "Hell-divers!" I looked up to see black enemy planes plummeting toward our ship.

CHAPTER 4

WARTIME LIFE
THE ALLIED HOME FRONTS

Like the First World War, the conflict of 1939-45 was a total war. It was fought directly by armed forces on battlefields, at sea and in the air. But civilians on the home fronts also felt its effects, and played an essential part in the long struggle for victory.

British civilians quickly adapted to the conflict. During the Phoney War (see page 20), about 1.5 million people, most of them children, were evacuated from London and other likely *Luftwaffe* targets. The children were placed with foster parents in country areas, but many returned home when no bombs fell. They were sent away again in the late summer of 1940 as the Blitz began. Civilians who stayed in the bombing zones built air-raid shelters at home and some served as ARP wardens (see page 23). A part-time, volunteer defence force was also formed on 14 May 1940, and soon became known as the Home Guard.

Women at work in a steel mill. In the war years, many British women carried out heavy industrial work that previously only men had done.

In January 1940, as U-boats sank food supply ships (see pages 24-5), the British government introduced rationing. At first it applied only to butter, sugar, ham and bacon, but soon other basic items were affected. People supplemented the food available in shops by growing vegetables. Many also bought supplies illegally on the black market.

Employment also came under government control and thousands of people were sent to work in factories that made weapons and military vehicles. As most British men aged 18-41 (later 51) were away fighting, much of the burden fell on women. From 1941, single women aged 21 to 31 had to join the armed forces or sign up for war work at home. Many were employed in industry. Others, known as Land Girls, went to work on farms as members of the Women's Land Army.

Civilians in the USA did not suffer air raids, but experienced the rationing of items such as petrol.

During air raids, many Londoners sheltered in the stations of the city's underground system. The platforms grew crowded and uncomfortable, but they were far safer than the streets and buildings above.

American industry, directed by a specially established War Production Board, contributed greatly to the war effort. Factories built to make military equipment included Ford Motor Company's Willow Run Complex, which mass-produced B-24 bombers. Under the terms of the Lend-Lease Act (see page 24), America supplied Britain and the USSR with weapons and vehicles. By 1944, nearly 30 per cent of British military equipment came from the USA.

America's wartime industrial growth brought the Depression to an end. However, as the new centres of employment rapidly attracted thousands of people, particularly African-Americans from the South, shortages of homes, schools and hospitals followed. War industries offered women opportunities for employment in new fields. By 1945, an extra 4 million had taken jobs.

R-556—Rev. 10-1-42

A

MILEAGE RATION

Americans had to use ration stamps like this to obtain gasoline (petrol).

SOVIET INDUSTRY

The people of the USSR endured terrible hardships during the Second World War. Starvation rations, poor housing and inadequate medical care all combined to make life almost intolerable. But in the midst of the chaos, Soviet industry staged a remarkable recovery after its evacuation to the Ural Mountains and beyond (see page 31). One tank factory was functioning again only 10 weeks after its move eastwards, and in 1944 the USSR produced nearly 29,000 armoured vehicles.

Nothing was wasted in wartime USSR. Here, Soviet engineers put captured Nazi tanks back together for use by their own armies.

Phyllis Bentley lived through the Second World War in Britain. In this extract from her book *O Dreams, O Destinations* (1962), she describes the many different types of work done by women during those years.

Ernest Bevin was the British Minister of Labour.

...how right **Ernest Bevin** was when he remarked later that the women tipped the scales of victory. It was not only that 7 million women in the armed forces, civil defence, agriculture and industry, packed the parachutes, typed the forms, drove the tractors and milked the cows, filled the shells, waterproofed the tanks, assembled the radio sets, kept the transport running, put out the incendiary bombs... But it was the ordinary housewife who was in fact decisive. She could have lost the war in any one week. Struggling to feed and clothe her family amid rations and coupons – meat and milk and butter and cheese and margarine and tea and sugar and eggs and soap were rationed, clothes and sweets could only be bought by coupons – if she had once revolted... the whole system would have become unworkable.

THE AXIS HOME FRONTS

The home fronts of the Axis Powers – Germany, Italy and Japan – were transformed just as much as those of the Allies. There, too, civilians suffered food shortages, coped with air raids and made weapons of war.

Adolf Hitler believed that Germany had lost the First World War because its army had been 'stabbed in the back' by civilians (see page 9). As a result, he was determined to keep morale high on the home front. In 1936, he began a Four-Year Plan to make the country self-sufficient in many foods and prevent the starvation that had killed thousands in 1918. Neverthless, rationing of meat and other items was introduced in 1939. By 1944, most items were rationed and people had little to eat.

Air raids on German cities began in 1940, and became regular events from 1942 (see page 53). As in Britain, an evacuation programme was set up to remove children from the danger zones. It was run by the *Hitlerjugend* (Hitler Youth), a Nazi group which all boys aged 10 to 18 had to join. Many evacuees moved to southern German states such as Bavaria.

Hitler did not fully mobilise the German economy for war in 1939. Many of the available factories were not taken over for military production and the output of armaments rose only slowly. The labour shortage caused by men's departure for the front

Members of the *Hitlerjugend* (Hitler Youth). A special section of this organisation was set up for young females aged 10 to 17, called the *Bund Deutscher Mädel* (Union of German Girls).

was, however, gradually solved by using slave workers from occupied territories.

Change came in 1942, as the Allies threatened German supremacy and Albert Speer became Minister for War Production. He quickly brought the economy under strict control and output soared. In 1940, German industry produced 2200 tanks. In 1944, 27,300 rolled off the assembly lines. By then, many women were employed in factories, as they had been ordered to register for war work in 1943. However, the Nazis believed that women's concerns should be mainly 'children, church and kitchen' and there was little pressure to take a job.

Under the rule of Benito Mussolini, wartime Italy

Nazi Minister for War Production Albert Speer tries out a new form of military transport. Speer was also an architect. He designed Germania, the grand capital that Hitler hoped would be built on the site of Berlin.

grew corrupt, disunited, and economically weak. Rationing was introduced to conserve food, but was badly run. Italian industry's attempts to contribute to the war effort were also poor. This was largely due to the government's inability to co-ordinate production and research, or to keep powerful companies such as Fiat under control. Shortage of raw materials was also a major problem. The output of tanks, aircraft and weapons always remained low, and there was little attempt to develop new technology.

JAPAN'S WAR

In 1938, the Japanese government passed the National Mobilisation Law, which gave it powers to prepare the country for war. In 1940, a network of local groups was set up to organise a wide range of activities such as civil defence. Two years later, the groups were given responsibility for distributing rations. The Japanese curriculum was adapted to meet the demands of war from 1941. Children learned about the importance of military activities and about the need to defend the emperor. When the bombing of Japanese cities began in earnest in 1944, many children were evacuated to the countryside. Japan's war production was small because of its limited raw materials. The country's inability to replace ships and aircraft lost in combat hastened its defeat.

Japanese evacuees crowd on to trains at Tokyo's Uyeno station.

Hitler would not tolerate any form of dissent. Special organisations such as the SS (an elite security force) and the Gestapo (secret police) spied on suspected opponents of the Nazi regime. The Bielenbergs (see page 17) opposed Hitler from the outset, as did many of their friends. In this extract from *The Past Is Myself*, Christabel Bielenberg records a discussion with her neighbour, Carl Langbehn, about the SS and its leader, Heinrich Himmler.

For information on the Nazis' racial theories, see pages 46-7.

This means that the SS did not take suspects to court, they just killed (liquidated) them.

Al Capone was a brutal American gangster of the 1920s.

...if it had not been Langbehn speaking, quietly, soberly, without emotion, I would not have been able to believe what he had to say about the SS... and of Himmler who, though he looked like the caricature of any village schoolmaster, was obsessed [with] fair-haired Nordic types. Everyone about him, his adjutants, his secretaries, had to be blonde and blue-eyed...The captains of his shining white knights [were cold] clever, utterly ruthless, interested purely in power for the sake of power, they ruled a State within a State, one which had no legal conscience, where the word 'liquidate' had replaced any conception of legality. It would be useless to appeal to their consciences – they had none. It was as if the Chicago underworld of Al Capone and his thugs had been let loose to run the country.

OCCUPATION AND RESISTANCE

Hitler aimed to create a New Order in German-occupied Europe. From France in the west to the USSR in the east, the land was to provide *Lebensraum*, slave labourers, raw materials and food for Germans.

The Nazis governed each nation under their control differently. Belgium and northern France were occupied and placed under military rule in 1940, while the Vichy regime (see page 21) was set up in southern France. German occupation was extended across France in 1942, but the Vichy government remained. Serbia (originally part of Yugoslavia) and parts of Greece were also ruled by Nazi military administrations.

Other countries were placed under civil (non-military) rule. After their monarchs went into exile, Norway and the Netherlands were ruled by partly independent local governments headed by Nazi officials. In Denmark, King Christian X ruled under strict Nazi supervision. Poland and most occupied areas of the USSR were directly and brutally governed by civil administrations.

The Germans controlled almost every aspect of life in lands under their rule, from education to employment. The

EUROPE IN 1942

Germany
German allies
Territory occupied by Germany
Neutral countries
Greater Germany

media were censored. Nazi officials supervised industry and agriculture and sent much of their output back to Germany. The economies of the occupied lands were left to collapse and their people to go hungry.

Groups in many occupied areas actively resisted German rule. The French resistance

After his country was occupied in 1940, French general Charles de Gaulle escaped to London and set up the Free French organisation. Its members were French soldiers determined to continue the fight against the Nazis. Here de Gaulle inspects a unit of Free French commandos.

movement developed in 1940. It helped Jews and Allied airmen who had crash-landed in France to escape, bombed factories, railways and bridges used by the Nazis, and intercepted their radio communications. Resistance was also strong in Denmark, and in 1943 a Freedom Council was set up which organised strikes and sabotage. In Yugoslavia, the anti-Nazi guerrilla warfare led by Marshal Tito was particularly effective. In 1940, the British set up the Special Operations Executive (SOE), which sent agents to support resistance movements abroad. The American equivalent, the Office of Strategic Services (OSS), was created in 1942.

The Nazi stranglehold on Europe was enforced by SS brutality. As a result, most people in occupied lands had to co-operate with some aspects of German rule that they found offensive. There were also a few willing collaborators, who actively supported the Nazis. They included Vidkun Quisling, leader of the Norwegian Fascist Party.

JAPANESE OCCUPATION

The Japanese brutally exploited the inhabitants of China's occupied areas from 1931. But people who lived in the lands that Japan captured after Pearl Harbor hoped for better. The Greater East Asia Co-Prosperity Sphere (see pages 36-7) was supposed to bring not only an end to Western colonial rule, but also economic success. Instead it brought domination by the Tokyo government and the diversion of precious raw materials to Japan. Thousands of Burmese and Thai civilians were forced to work in appalling conditions to build the infamous Burma Railway, a vital communications link. Europeans were interned in squalid camps. Any resistance was fiercely crushed by the *Kempeitai*, the Japanese secret police.

Many resistance workers paid for their courage with their lives. Among them was a young Dane called Kim Malthe-Bruun. In 1941, he had become a merchant seaman, and on his travels had witnessed the Nazis' terrible treatment of the Jews. He joined the Danish resistance in 1944, but was captured the next year. These extracts come from his prison diary. They take the form of letters to his girlfriend, Hanne.

This is equal to approximately 1.9m by 1.2m.

21 March, 1945

...
The cell I had when I sat in Detention was on the small side – 6 feet, 3 inches by 4 feet – with a small bench and a table. I walked up and down – one and a half paces in each direction; twenty-four hours and all alike, only broken by the opening of the door when two slices of rye bread were handed to me... In the toilet they allowed me to wash, and it was wonderful. Then I paced up and down again, very much surprised that I didn't suffer. I thought of the days spent in solitary confinement and how rewarding they had been. I had the sun, the blue sky... I could smell the earth and feel the coming of spring. It made me choke up inside and I felt very happy... I'm kept going by one thought: that nothing is impossible no matter how black things look at the moment.

4 April 1945

...
Today I was taken before the military tribunal and condemned to death.

Kim Malthe-Bruun, aged 18

THE HOLOCAUST

Anti-Semitism (hatred and persecution of Jews) was widespread in Europe long before Hitler came to power. However, the Nazis set out to achieve something never before contemplated – the extermination of the entire Jewish people. They failed, but not before approximately 6 million Jews had been murdered in the tragedy of the Holocaust.

In Hitler's mind, Jews were worthy of hatred for many reasons, but he blamed them in particular for Germany's First World War defeat. He also thought that they were racially inferior *Untermenschen* (subhumans), like Slavs. By contrast, he believed in the existence of a superior Aryan race. Its supposed members were all white, often with blonde hair and blue eyes.

As soon as the Nazis came to power, the persecution of Jews began. In 1933, laws were passed banning them from many types of employment, including the professions and military service. The 1935 Nuremberg Laws denied Jews the right to be German citizens and to vote. They also made it illegal for Jews to marry Germans. Then, on 9-10 November 1938, came *Kristallnacht* (the Night of Broken Glass). Thousands of houses and shops owned by Jews were destroyed, and hundreds of synagogues set on fire. Many Jews were arrested and sent to concentration camps.

By the time the war began, thousands of German Jews had emigrated. For those who remained, the persecution intensified. Meanwhile, more sinister developments were taking place in the newly occupied territories. In Poland, many Jews were killed outright and the rest were forced to live together in special areas, known as ghettos. After the German invasion of the USSR in 1941, SS *Einsatzgruppen* (Special Action Units) went in after the armies to kill Jews, as well as Communist leaders. Thousands of people were shot, or poisoned with carbon monoxide in gas vans. But still there was worse to come.

In July 1941, Nazi leader Hermann Goering issued a directive in which he ordered SS officer Reinhard Heydrich to submit a plan for the 'Final Solution' of the Jewish question. In January 1942, Heydrich and Adolf Eichmann, another SS officer, agreed plans for the annihilation of 11 million Jews. Existing concentration camps such as Auschwitz were to be equipped with gas chambers, and new death camps to be built in places such as Treblinka. The mass killings began soon after. The fit were worked to death. All others were gassed, for example with Zyklon B.

Since the war, historians have argued about who was responsible for the Holocaust. Hitler and other high-ranking Nazis were certainly aware of what was happening. So, too, were camp staff. But how much the general German public and the wider world knew of the Jews' suffering remains the subject of debate.

After *Kristallnacht* in November 1938, some Germans pause to examine the damage caused to Jewish-owned property. Others simply avert their gaze.

Nazi soldiers force Jews out of the ghetto in Warsaw, the capital of Poland, in 1943. The small boy with his hands up is believed to have died in the concentration camp at Auschwitz.

FELLOW SUFFERERS

Hitler and his Nazi followers did not persecute only Jews. Thousands of gypsies, homosexuals and political prisoners died in concentration camps. In addition, about 70,000 people with hereditary illnesses, children as well as adults, were killed at special euthanasia centres. These were set up after a Euthanasia Order was passed in October 1939.

 Eva Heyman was a 13-year-old Jewish girl who lived in Budapest, the capital of Hungary. In these extracts from her diary, she tells how the city's Jews were first herded into a ghetto, then deported. In October 1944, Eva and her grandparents were killed in Auschwitz.

This order was introduced elsewhere as early as 1939.

March 31, 1944

Today an order was issued that from now on Jews have to wear a yellow star-shaped patch. The order tells exactly how big the star patch must be, and that it must be sewn on every outer garment...

May 5, 1944

Dear diary, now you aren't... at home... but in the Ghetto. Three days we waited for them to come and get us... The city was divided into sections, and a German truck would wait in front of the houses and two policemen would go into the apartments and bring the people out...

May 29, 1944

And so, dear diary, now the end of everything has really come. The Ghetto has been divided up into blocks and we're all going to be taken away from here.

 After the war, many Nazis were brought to justice at the Nuremberg War Crimes Trials, which were held from November 1945 to September 1946.

The following extract comes from an interview given to the official American psychologist at the trials by Auschwitz commandant SS Colonel Rudolf Hoess.

The bodies of the dead were cremated in huge ovens.

I asked Hoess how it was technically possible to exterminate 2½ million people. 'Technically?' he asked. 'That wasn't so hard...it was possible to exterminate up to 10,000 people in one 24-hour period... The killing itself took the least time... it was the burning that took all the time. The killing was easy; you didn't even need guards to drive them into the chambers; they just went in expecting to take showers and, instead of water, we turned on poison gas. The whole thing went very quickly.' He related all this in a quiet, apathetic, matter-of-fact tone of voice.

PRISONERS OF WAR

Records do not show exactly how many members of the Allied and Axis armed forces were captured in the Second World War, but it may have been as many as 15 million. Some fell into enemy hands alone; others surrendered in their thousands. All faced uncertain futures as prisoners of war (POWs).

The treatment of prisoners of war was regulated by various international agreements. Among them was the Geneva Convention of 1929, which gave prisoners the right to receive food, drink and medical care, to withhold all information except name, rank and number, and to receive letters and parcels.

The British and Americans took more than 1 million prisoners of war, over half of them German. Some were shipped to the USA and Canada. Many North American camps were specially built in agricultural areas so that prisoners could be employed as farm labourers. After D-Day (see pages 50-1),

The ominous-looking Colditz Castle, a POW camp that stood near the German city of Leipzig. Some POWs did manage to escape from its high-security facilities.

many were also sent to the 86 camps scattered all over the United Kingdom. In general, men held in these countries were treated well.

The USSR was far less scrupulous about its conduct towards prisoners of war. Information is scarce, but experts believe it ran about 3000 prison camps. There, millions of Germans and others were ill-fed and treated with the utmost cruelty. Some prisoners never reached the camps. In one terrible incident that took place in 1940 in the Katyn Forest, near Smolensk, Russia, about 4000 Polish soldiers were massacred by the Soviet security police.

The Germans acted differently towards different groups of prisoners. Their 5 million Soviet captives were regarded as Slav 'subhumans' and treated accordingly. Many were shot and others were worked to death. Only about 1.5 million survived the war. British, American and other prisoners were usually sent to camps. There were about 90 camps in Germany, and more in occupied areas such as Poland.

The Japanese took about 145,000 prisoners of war and distributed them in some 700 camps throughout their empire. All were treated with barbarity and neglect (see document page 49). Men were fed starvation rations, yet expected to carry out back-breaking physical labour. Medical care was basic or non-existent. Thousands of prisoners died.

This column of dejected Soviet POWs stretches as far as the eye can see. The soldiers faced extreme cruelty at the hands of their Nazi captors.

Bohdan Arct was one of many Polish Air Force officers who escaped after the fall of Poland in 1939, then served with the Allies. In 1944, Arct was captured and sent to a prison camp in Germany. While in captivity, Arct compiled a logbook. The two pages (right) and the extract (below) are taken from it.

I was then showed to my future "home", Barracks No 11... Cold, overcrowded and with no indoor conveniences, it had to accommodate sixteen people in one room the size of [a] medium bedroom. We had double bunks instead of beds and wooden boards instead of springs... The whole camp... was divided into several compounds... On one end of the compound there was a huge barrack for kitchen, church and theatre... On the other end we had parade grounds...

After the fall of Singapore (see page 37), Eric
Lomax was imprisoned by the Japanese. At first he was placed in a 'good' camp, but after he was found to have a radio and a railway map, he was brutally beaten and moved into a prison 'hutch'. These extracts from *The Railway Man* (see page 19) describe both experiences.

ENEMY ALIENS

Not all wartime prisoners were members of the armed forces. Many were civilians who, after war broke out, found themselves living in countries that regarded them as enemies. Many thousands of Germans and other 'enemy aliens' were sent to internment camps in Britain, but by the summer of 1942 only about 5000 remained under guard. In the USA, there were about 110,000 Japanese-Americans living on the Pacific coast. In 1942, all were imprisoned in detention centres, although many were released before the end of the war. Some joined the US armed forces and became highly respected and much decorated troops.

Our single long hut could hold about a hundred men and was little more than ingenious tents made from local vegetation... The floor was trodden earth... but under each bed-space was still raw clay, which sprouted even in the dark... The cool dark spaces also sheltered wriggling and crawling life, of which the most terrifying were scorpions and snakes...

The left-hand side of the yard was bounded by a wall; and along part of its length were blocks of little hutch-like cells or cages. They resembled drawers in a filing cabinet. We were each ushered into one of these cells through a small, low door about two feet square... I lay down on the floor, diagonally... I had to lie cramped, my arms held up to prevent my own weight crushing the unset bones...

One foot equals about 30cm.

A beating had left Lomax with broken forearms.

THE ROAD TO VICTORY OPERATION OVERLORD

By 1943, Allied victories in North Africa (see pages 26-7) and Stalingrad (see pages 32-3) had overshadowed the Germans' early *Blitzkrieg* triumphs. Next, Britain and the USA planned to bring the war back to Western Europe, and to deal Hitler a final crushing blow.

The Americans had long wished to open a Second Front in France. However, British prime minister Winston Churchill, fearful of another Dunkirk (see page 21), did not want to proceed until he was certain of success. In January 1943, Churchill met President Roosevelt at a conference in Casablanca. There he persuaded the Americans to invade the Italian island of Sicily (see box). But the Soviets, who had also been calling for a new Western Front to ease the pressure on the Eastern Front, joined the USA in pushing for action. Finally, Churchill agreed to aim for an invasion of France,

codename Operation Overlord, in May 1944.

Over the following months, the invasion was planned in precise detail. American general Dwight D. Eisenhower, the Supreme Allied Commander in overall charge of the operation, worked closely with British general Bernard Montgomery (see page 21), who was to lead the forces on the ground. By early 1944, the basic outline of Overlord was clear. British, American and Canadian troops were to land on five beaches in Normandy, northwest France (see map), from the sea and from the air. The invasion was to begin on 5 June: D-Day.

In the event, bad weather caused a delay and the D-Day landings began on 6 June. About 23,000 paratroopers went in first, followed by 130,000 men in five divisions on the ground. The American forces at Omaha Beach faced strong resistance, but finally got ashore like everyone else.

OPERATION OVERLORD

American soldiers make their way through the water to the Normandy coast. The invasion fleet ships (in the background) were too large to come up to the beach.

Careful planning, courageous fighting and a disinformation campaign which persuaded the Germans that the invasion was planned to land near Calais, not in Normandy, made Operation Overlord a success.

Thousands more Allied troops crossed the English Channel over the following weeks. Meanwhile, armies led by Montgomery and American generals Omar Bradley and George Patton set out to break the German defences in Normandy. This took longer than expected, but, on 16 August, Hitler ordered his troops to retreat and the Allies moved across northern France. Paris was liberated by a Franco-American force on 25 August. In a separate development on 15 August, American and French troops had landed on France's south coast and made their way north. Victory was in sight, but it would not be sealed for some time to come.

THE ITALIAN CAMPAIGN

The Allied invasion of Sicily was launched from North Africa in July 1943. Over the next month, the Italians and Germans were forced to retreat, but many escaped to mainland Italy. Meanwhile, Italian king Victor Emmanuel III had forced Mussolini to resign. On 3 September, the Italian government signed an armistice with the Allies, but Mussolini set up a separate German-backed government in the north. The Allies invaded Italy from the southern port of Salerno on 9 September. They made slow progress and further landings at Anzio in January 1944 did little to help. In May, Allied troops finally took the long-contested hilltop site of Monte Cassino. Rome fell on 4 June and the Germans retreated north, but the Allies did not achieve complete victory until May 1945. By then Mussolini was dead. He had been shot by Italians in April while fleeing to Switzerland.

Elliott Johnson served with the American Fourth Infantry Division. On 6 June 1944 he arrived in Normandy by sea, as he recalls in this account taken from Studs Terkel's *"The Good War"* (see page 37).

I was on an LST, a landing ship tank. It was three hundred feet long. It had a great mouth in front of which was the ramp that let down the smaller craft. I remember going up to the highest part of that ship and watching the panorama around me unfold. In my mind's eye, I see one of our ships take a direct hit and go up in a huge ball of flames. There were big geysers coming up where the shells were landing and there were bodies floating, face down, face up. The LST, as we vacated it, was to become a hospital ship. The boys who had gone first and been wounded were now being brought out...

VICTORY IN EUROPE

While British and American troops were threatening Germany from the west, the Red Army was keeping up the relentless pressure from the east. By the winter of 1944, Hitler's forces were dangerously trapped in the ever-narrowing gap between them.

Soviet troops had not ceased to move west since their success at the Battle of Kursk in July 1943 (see page 33). In the first half of 1944 they ended the terrible siege of Leningrad (see page 30) and recaptured the Ukraine and the Crimea. On 22 June, they launched a new offensive, Operation Bagration, that pushed the Germans into Poland. Then, in August, the Red Army began a campaign in the Balkans that temporarily halted the Soviet drive westwards.

In the west, the British and Americans were still making progress, but not without difficulty. In September 1944, a plan to invade Germany from the Netherlands failed. Then, on 16 December, the Germans launched a surprise counter-offensive through the Ardennes region of Belgium and Luxembourg. At first the Germans were able to push forwards, creating a bulge in their front line. But the Allied recovery was swift, and in the Battle of the Bulge, the German salient was eliminated. By the end of January 1945, the Allies were forging eastwards once more.

In February, General Eisenhower (see page 50) launched the Rhineland Campaign. His armies were to cross the River Rhine, then defeat Hitler's forces in the Ruhr region of Germany. American troops led by General Patton made the crossing on 22 March, with British troops under Montgomery following the next day. The Germans were encircled and on 18 April, 400,000 surrendered. Eisenhower then sent troops to wipe out remaining German resistance.

The Red Army launched a new onslaught against the Nazis on 12 January 1945. First it powered into Poland, taking Warsaw five days into the offensive. Then it continued west, reaching the River Oder, just 60km from Berlin, by the end of February. Troops showed no mercy to civilians, killing and raping as they advanced. The build-up of Soviet forces continued until 16 April, when Marshal Zhukov (see page 30) began his attack on the German capital. Fighting was fierce, but by 25 April the city was surrounded. Hitler committed suicide on 30 April and Berlin surrendered two days later. The Germans signed a full unconditional surrender on 7 May. The war in Europe was over.

In this dramatic scene, a Soviet soldier hoists the Red Flag of the USSR above the captured city of Berlin. The devastation caused by the last-ditch struggle for the German capital can be seen below.

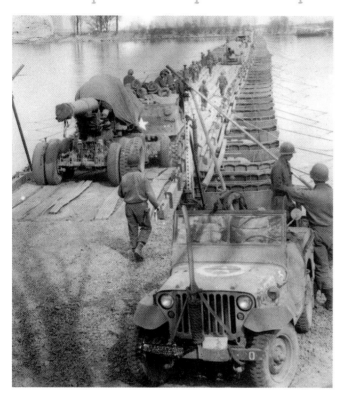

This bridge across the Rhine was built by engineers of the American Third Army.

 Many Allied troops made the Rhine crossing by raft. Here British lieutenant Derrick Vernon of the Royal Engineers describes the scene.

Good watermanship was required to drive the raft across the wide fast-flowing river. Each platoon operated for sixteen hours non-stop. Two rafts were maintained constantly in service, signal lamps were placed for continued operation throughout the night... When ordered to cease operations we were very tired. In three days, the company had made about seven hundred round trips across a very dangerous river in flimsy craft. We suffered nine men killed in action, and twenty wounded.

 Janina Bauman was a young Jewish woman who managed to survive in Poland until the war's end. In this extract from her book, *Winter In The Morning* (1986), she describes the arrival of Soviet troops in her village on their way to Berlin.

Cracow is a Polish city.

The Red Army was now heading westwards with unbelievable speed. On the day that the long-awaited battle of Warsaw finally began, we also heard the first sounds of the Eastern Front approaching Cracow... For us the war came to an abrupt end at 8 a.m. on Friday, 19 January 1945. After a sleepless night echoing with cannon-fire, heavy with great expectations, we saw in the faint light of the wintry dawn the weird, grey hunched outlines of the first Russian soldiers.

Janina Bauman, aged 11

VICTORY IN THE PACIFIC

By mid-1943, after defeats at the Battle of Midway and Guadalcanal (see pages 38-9), the Japanese were on the defensive in the Pacific. Their fierce resistance to the American advance on Japan itself led to the employment of a new and horrific weapon of war.

The Americans launched a two-pronged offensive against the Japanese. General Douglas MacArthur was to take New Guinea and the Philippines. Admiral Chester Nimitz was to drive the enemy from the small island groups in the Central Pacific. The assault on New Guinea began in September and by early 1944, the Americans were in control of the island. Nimitz began his attacks in November 1943 and by mid-1944, the Gilbert, Marshall, Caroline and Mariana islands were also in American hands. American forces secured a victory in Saipan, one of the Mariana islands, by winning the Battle of the Philippine Sea in June.

THE WAR IN THE PACIFIC 1944-5

Allied attacks
Nuclear explosion
Major naval battles
1 Philippine Sea, June 1944
2 Leyte Gulf, October 1944

In July 1944, President Roosevelt, MacArthur and Nimitz met to decide the American forces' next move. Roosevelt ordered Nimitz to work with MacArthur for the reconquest of the Philippines.

Air strikes on the islands began shortly afterwards. Then, on 20 October, American troops landed on Leyte (see map). The Japanese navy responded by attacking the American fleet. The Battle of Leyte Gulf, on 23-6 October, ended with the withdrawal of the Japanese and the collapse of their naval threat to the USA. Combat on the islands was also intense. Manila, the Philippine capital, did not fall until March 1945.

By early 1945, the Americans were hoping to force a Japanese surrender. The nearby islands of Iwo Jima and Okinawa were taken in the spring. At the same

The devastated landscape of Hiroshima after the atomic bomb fell

time, air raids on Tokyo by B-29 bombers were intensified. However, it became obvious that Japan was not going to surrender, and might have to be invaded. Allied leaders knew that Japanese soldiers would fight to the death to resist invasion. The casualty figures would reach the hundreds of thousands.

There was another option. Scientists working on the secret Manhattan Project in the USA had developed an atomic bomb. It was believed to be so terrible a weapon it could force a surrender. Roosevelt had died in April, so new President Harry S. Truman had to decide whether to use this weapon. He gave his approval and a message was sent to Japan on 27 July demanding surrender or threatening to use the bomb. The message was ignored. On 6 August, a bomb was dropped on the city of Hiroshima. About 80,000 people were killed, but Japan's government did not capitulate. On 9 August another bomb was dropped on Nagasaki. Five days later, Emperor Hirohito announced Japan's surrender. The Second World War had ended.

BACK TO BURMA

The British also fought to regain territories that they had lost to Japan. Among them was Burma. Lieutenant General Sir William Slim launched his offensive from the north in December 1944. As his troops moved south they met strong resistance, but by May 1945 had taken the country's capital, Rangoon.

During the Battle of Leyte Gulf and on many other occasions, Japanese *kamikaze* pilots flew their aeroplanes into enemy ships. They chose their deaths for the honour of Japan. This extract comes from a letter written by *kamikaze* pilot Akio Otsuka.

11.30 a.m. – the last morning. I shall now have breakfast and then go to the aerodrome. I am busy with my final briefing and have no time to write any more. So I bid you farewell...

Keep in good health.

I believe in the victory of Greater Asia.

I pray for the happiness of you all, and I beg your forgiveness for my lack of piety.

I leave for the attack with a smile on my face. The moon will be full to-night. As I fly over the open sea off Okinawa I will choose the enemy ship that is to be my target.

I will show you that I know how to die bravely.

A young *kamikaze* pilot in July 1944

American writer John Hersey wrote *Hiroshima* in 1946, a year after the atomic bomb fell on that city. His book contains the stories of six men and women who survived the explosion and its aftermath. The following extract recalls the experiences of Reverend Mr Kiyoshi Tanimoto, pastor of the local Methodist Church.

He was the only person making his way into the city; he met hundreds and hundreds who were fleeing, and every one of them seemed to be hurt in some way. The eyebrows of some were burned off and skin hung from their faces and hands. Others, because of pain, held their arms up as if carrying something in both hands. Some were vomiting as they walked. Many were naked or in shreds of clothing...

THE POST-WAR WORLD

Even before the Second World War ended in Europe, the Allies had begun to plan the continent's future. During their discussions, it had become clear that the democratic Western Allies (Britain and the USA) had little in common with their Communist partner, the USSR. Immediately after the war, as the three nations struggled to create a workable framework for peace, the divisions between them grew.

The first major conference to discuss the post-war world took place in February 1945 at Yalta in the Crimea. The main participants were US President Franklin D. Roosevelt, British Prime Minister Winston Churchill and the Soviet leader Joseph Stalin. They decided that Germany and its capital Berlin would be divided into four zones, each controlled by a separate country (the USA, Britain, the USSR and France). They also agreed to set up a new peace-keeping organisation, the United Nations. In addition, they declared that all of the newly liberated nations had the right to choose their own form of government.

More discussions took place at the July 1945 Potsdam Conference in Germany. By then much had changed. The war in Europe was over and the Red Army was camped on vast eastern areas of the continent. Roosevelt had been succeeded by

POST-WAR EUROPE

Territory annexed by USSR 1940-5

Territory under Soviet control by 1948

'Iron Curtain'

Other countries with Communist governments

0   200 miles
0   300 km

Finland, Sweden, Denmark, Estonia, Latvia, Lithuania, East Prussia, Former Polish territory, USSR, Former Romanian territory, Poland, East Germany, West Germany, Czechoslovakia, Austria, Hungary, Romania, Yugoslavia, Bulgaria, Italy, Albania, Greece, Turkey, Baltic Sea

Truman, who thought that Communism was a threat to the West. New British prime minister Clement Attlee replaced Churchill in mid-conference. Some decisions were reached under these difficult conditions, for example on the future borders of Poland and the establishment of war crimes trials. However, the wish of the USSR to stop free elections in Eastern Europe caused serious clashes.

After Potsdam, the stresses in the relationship between the USSR and its former Allies increased,

The 'Big Three' – Winston Churchill, Franklin D. Roosevelt and Joseph Stalin – at the Yalta Conference in February 1945 as Stalin imposed his will on one East European state after another. In 1946, Churchill declared that an 'Iron Curtain' – a divide between democratic West and Communist East – had descended across the continent. By 1948, Bulgaria, Hungary, Romania, Poland and Czechoslovakia were all under Soviet control. Communists were also in power in Albania and Yugoslavia.

In 1947, President Truman moved to counteract the Soviet threat. In March, he declared his intention to support any country trying to resist Communist rule. This declaration was later called the Truman Doctrine. It stated that 'It must be the policy of the United States to support free peoples who are resisting attempted subjugation by armed minorities or by outside pressure.' Although no direct mention of Communism is made, the reference is clear. Concerned that Europe's post-war economic problems would lead even nations such as France and Italy to embrace Communism, Truman also set up the Marshall Plan. This $17 billion aid package was named after US Secretary of State George C. Marshall.

The two sides had staked their claims. Their battles were political and intellectual, not physical. The era of the Cold War had begun.

WAR REFUGEES

After the war, great tides of refugees swept across Europe. Millions had fled in front of the advancing Allied armies. Millions more Germans had been driven out of the liberated territories. There were also many Poles, who had lost their lands to Russia in the east. Jews who had survived the death camps and slave labourers who had worked in German factories all struggled to find their way back to their different homelands. The cost in human misery was high.

Hungarian refugees make their way home from Slovakia, where they had worked as slave labourers for the Nazis.

In his memoirs, Field-Marshal Viscount Bernard Montgomery (see page 21) details the many problems that faced the Allied armies in Germany after the fighting was over, in particular the presence of millions of refugees.

After the war, Berliners struggled to repair bomb damage in their city.

In the area occupied by 21 Army Group there were appalling civilian problems to be solved. Over 1 million civilian refugees had fled into the area before the advancing Russians. About 1 million German wounded were in hospital in the area, with no medical supplies. Over 1.5 million unwounded German fighting men had surrendered to 21 Army Group on the 5th May and were now prisoners of war... Food would shortly be exhausted. The transport and communication services had ceased to function, and industry and agriculture were largely at a standstill. The population had to be fed, housed and kept free of disease. It was going to be a race for time whether this could be achieved before the winter began...

CONCLUSION

The Second World War outdid even the First in its scope and brutality. The fighting raged across six continents and killed up to 60 million people, more of them civilians than combatants. Over a third of the casualties came from just one country, the USSR. The atrocity of the Holocaust added another inhuman dimension to the conflict.

In the aftermath, the world was transformed. The USA and USSR took their places as the new superpowers and confronted each other in the Cold War for the next 40 years. Britain, France, Germany and many other European countries rebuilt their ruined cities and economies with the help of Marshall Aid. Japan slowly recovered from the loss of its empire to become an economically powerful nation. Many Jews left Europe to make homes in Israel, which was established in 1948.

Today the war is still remembered and its effects are still felt. Many of those who fought in the conflict attend annual remembrance services, and sometimes return to the battle zones. Slave labourers who worked for the Nazis are still struggling to get compensation from the German government. Jewish organisations continue to track down the few surviving concentration camp officials and high-ranking Nazis who have escaped justice. The Japanese are still suffering the dreadful consequences of the atomic bombs dropped on Hiroshima and Nagasaki. For these people, the war remains a constant part of life.

Since the Second World War, there have been hundreds of armed conflicts around the world, but none on the same scale. The United Nations Organisation, established in 1945 to preserve peace (see document), still works to prevent a repetition of that terrible event, which cost so many millions of lives and ruined so many more.

In 1961, a wall was built through Berlin to separate the Communist east of the city from the democratic, capitalist west. The wall became a symbol of the Cold War. In the same way, its destruction in 1989 (below) was a sign that this bitter conflict was coming to an end.

Austrian Nazi Adolf Eichmann played a major part in the attempted extermination of the Jews. He disappeared after the war, but was discovered and captured by Israeli agents in 1960. A year later he stood trial in Israel for his war crimes, was found guilty and executed.

Many soldiers who participated in the Second World War remember it with mixed emotions. Often they were fighting for what they believed was right, yet still found it terrible to kill and maim their fellow humans. In these extracts, British soldier James Bramwell and Jewish American surgeon Dr Alex Shulman express their thoughts on the conflict. The second extract comes from _"The Good War"_ (see page 37).

When he was mounting his final defence, Hitler recruited boys and old men into his armies because there were not enough men of fighting age left.

I shudder at the thought of war, but men are more evil than I had realised... War is the crunch of big ideas and taking sides is terribly difficult. But it has to be done; and you have to have the idea as you take your side, you're going to prevail. You have to be sure yours is the right side. They are almost religious decisions... War is a kind of uplift to some people. In war you see humanity at the end of its tether, so you know what the human being is capable of. I had moments of feeling cheerful. I wasn't wasting four years of my life.

I'm glad I participated. I felt that whatever little I did was something. My job was to save lives. I was asked, How could you take care of those Germans? Doesn't that bother you? Oh, I started looking at them at first as Germans and Nazis. Then I started looking at them as victims. Especially at the end, when I saw the kids and the old men. Could I blame that kid for what his parents or the Nazi leaders did? It was a terrible, mixed feeling. Why shouldn't I take care of a sixteen-year-old kid that's been shot to pieces?

 The following extract is taken from the Charter of the United Nations, which was adopted on 25 June 1945.

The United Nations Building in New York City, USA

We the Peoples of the United Nations determined
   to save succeeding generations from the scourge of war, which twice in our lifetime has brought untold sorrow to mankind, and
   to reaffirm faith in fundamental human rights, in the dignity and worth of the human person, in the equal rights of men and women and of nations large and small...
and for these ends
   to practise tolerance and live together in peace with one another as good neighbours, and
   to unite our strength to maintain international peace and security, and
   to ensure, by the acceptance of principles and the institution of methods, that armed force shall not be used, save in the common interest...
have resolved to combine our efforts to accomplish these aims

GLOSSARY

Afrika Korps The German army that served in North Africa from February 1941 to May 1943.

Allies The 49 countries that fought together against the Axis Powers. The main Allies were Great Britain, France, the USA and the USSR. Many British Commonwealth countries, for example Australia and India, also fought on the Allied side.

annex To add a territory to one's own land by using military force.

Anschluss The annexation of Austria by the Nazis in 1938.

anti-Semitism Prejudice against and persecution of Jews.

appeasement The policy of giving in to the demands of a potential enemy in an effort to maintain peace.

armistice An official agreement between opposing sides to stop fighting in a war.

Aryan A member of a supposed white race that the Nazis thought was superior to all others.

Axis Powers The eight countries that fought together against the Allies. The main Axis Powers were Germany and Italy, who formed the Rome-Berlin Axis in 1936, and Japan, who signed the Tripartite Pact with them in 1940.

Balkans A peninsula in southeastern Europe that in the Second World War contained the countries of Albania, Bulgaria, Greece, Romania, Yugoslavia and the European part of Turkey.

Blitzkrieg ('lightning war') A Nazi method of attack, designed to overwhelm enemies with its speed and force. It usually began with paratroop drops and aerial bombing, then continued with tank and infantry invasions.

British Expeditionary Force The first British troops that went to France to participate in the war.

capitalism An economic system in which businesses are owned and run by private individuals for their own profit rather than by the state.

Central Powers The countries that fought against the Allies in the First World War. They were Austria-Hungary, Germany, the Ottoman (Turkish) Empire and Bulgaria.

Chancellor The head of the German government.

coalition government A government made up of more than one political party.

Communism A political and economic system that aims to create a classless society in which everyone has a fair share of money and power. Communist countries are ruled by members of one political party, who are not elected. Communist businesses are run by the state rather than by private individuals.

concentration camps Camps where large numbers of people are held prisoner. In some Nazi concentration camps, such as Auschwitz and Treblinka, about 6 million Jews, as well as many gypsies, homosexuals and political prisoners, were killed in gas chambers.

conscription Compulsory service in the armed forces.

convoys A group of merchant ships escorted by navy warships for protection from U-boat attacks.

coup A violent overthrow of a government.

democracy A form of government in which all the adults of a country elect the politicans who rule over them.

Eastern Front The areas of Eastern Europe where opposing armies fought each other during the First and Second World Wars.

Entente Cordiale ('friendly understanding') The agreement formed between Britain and France in 1904.

Fascism A political belief characterised by extreme nationalism, strong leadership and opposition to both democracy and Communism.

Freikorps Groups of men who acted as security forces in Germany after the First World War.

front An area of a battle zone where opposing troops face and fight one another directly.

Führer ('leader') The title adopted by Adolf Hitler in 1934.

Gestapo The Nazi secret police force, set up in 1933. The name is short for Ge*heime Staatspolizei*, which means 'Secret State Police'.

ghettos The areas in European cities such as Warsaw where the Nazis forced Jews to live.

Great Depression The period of high unemployment and economic weakness after the Wall Street Crash of 1929.

Holocaust The mass murder of about 6 million Jews by the Nazis.

inflation A continual increase in the price of goods.

internment Holding in custody, for example in a prison or camp.

Lebensraum ('living space') The term used by Hitler to describe the territories that he occupied, claiming that they provided the space necessary for German people to flourish.

Maginot Line A line of forts and other defences built by the French. The main part ran along the German border from Switzerland to Luxembourg.

mandate A conquered territory governed by a member country of the League of Nations.

mobilise To assemble (troops) and prepare them for military action.

Nazi Party The National Socialist German Workers' Party. 'Nazi' is a short form of the German words for 'National Socialist'.

Nazi-Soviet Pact An agreement signed by Germany and the USSR in 1939 in which they promised not to attack each other.

Pact of Steel The official military alliance signed by Germany and Italy in May 1939.

paratroopers Troops that drop into battle zones by parachute.

plebiscite A direct vote taken by all the people of a country to decide an issue of national importance.

purge An act of eliminating political and other opponents, often by murdering them.

putsch A swift and violent revolt, usually designed to overthrow a government.

Red Army The army of the USSR, so called because it fought under the country's red flag.

Reichstag The name given to both the German parliament and its building in Berlin.

reparations Compensation, especially the compensation for the First World War demanded from Germany in the Treaty of Versailles.

Rome-Berlin Axis The unwritten alliance between Mussolini's Italy and Nazi Germany that began in 1936. It was officially confirmed when the two countries signed the Pact of Steel in 1939.

sanctions Actions taken against a state in an effort to punish it for illegal conduct or to make it act in a particular way, such as a ban on or reduction of exports.

Second Front The European fighting front that opened in France in June 1944, following Operation Overlord.

Serbs A Slav people who speak Serbo-Croat.

Slavs A group of peoples from eastern Europe and northwest Asia who speak Slavonic languages such as Russian, Polish and Serbo-Croat.

SS A Nazi security force led by Heinrich Himmler. Its name is short for the German word *Schutzstaffel*, which means 'protection squad'. The special *Waffen-SS* fought on the front lines.

strategic bombing Aerial bombing designed to hit specific targets as part of a war-winning strategy, rather than supporting troops on the ground.

Sturmabteilung (SA) ('storm division') The Nazis' private terrorist army, led until 1934 by Ernst Röhm. Its members were known as Brownshirts because of their uniforms.

tactical bombing Aerial bombing designed to support attacks by troops on the ground.

Third Reich Germany from 1933 to 1945. The Nazis believed that theirs was the third German Reich (empire) because it followed the Holy Roman Empire of the Middle Ages and the second empire of 1871 to 1918.

Tripartite Pact The pact signed by Germany, Italy and Japan in September 1940. In it, they agreed to defend one another in case of enemy attack. Romania, Bulgaria and Yugoslavia joined the pact later.

Triple Alliance The alliance formed by Austria-Hungary, Germany and Italy in 1882.

Triple Entente The alliance formed by Britain, France and Russia in 1907, during the run-up to the First World War.

Untermenschen The German word for 'subhumans'. The Nazis used it to refer to peoples that they considered inferior, such as Jews and Slavs.

Weimar Republic The republic that existed in Germany from 1919 to 1933, so called because its government first met in the town of Weimar.

Western Allies Britain, the USA and other Second World War Allies from Western capitalist countries.

Western Front The areas of Western Europe where opposing armies fought each other during the First and Second World Wars.

INDEX